MANAGING ARCHITECTURAL AND ENGINEERING PRACTICE

MANAGING ARCHITECTURAL AND ENGINEERING PRACTICE

WELD COXE

A Wiley- Interscience Publication

JOHN WILEY & SONS New York • Chichester • Brisbane • Toronto

Published by John Wiley & Sons, Inc.

Copyright © 1980 by Weld Coxe

Library of Congress Cataloging in Publication Data:
Coxe, Weld.
    Managing architectural and engineering practice.

    "A Wiley-Interscience publication."
    Includes index.
    1. Architectural practice—Management.   2. Engi-
neering—Management.   I. Title.
NA1996.C59   720'.68   80-17196
ISBN 0-471-08203-1

Printed in the United States of America

10 9 8 7 6 5 4 3 2 1

PREFACE

A generation ago, the concept of management as a component of professional design practice was virtually unheard of. After all, architecture is claimed to be the mother of all arts, and engineers, lawyers, doctors, and a legion of other "learned professions" have existed for centuries. By definition, these professions have "practices" for the benefit of their clients. Only since the mid-1960s have a sizable number of professional practices evolved into organizations having a life of their own—independent of service to clients—and deserving the kind of care and feeding that the discipline of management can provide.

I have been privileged to participate in this evolution, first as a nondiscipline staff member of a large design firm (Vincent G. Kling and Partners) and, since 1967, as a consultant to design professionals. At that time there were only two other firms specializing in the management of architectural and engineering practices. Today there are dozens, and even a special newsletter devoted to the subject. More significantly, the interest of in-house practitioners in the management of their firms has led to the formation of a separate professional society, the Professional Services Management Association, with some 800 members.

All of these are contributing to the evolving art of managing professional organizations. It is a different art, in significant respects, from the management of a business, and there is much more that will be learned as the field grows. I believe, however, that enough is now known about the special nature of managing design practice so that it is timely to summarize the state of the art.

This book is intended as a handbook for all managers of design practice, whether they be professional architects or engineers who have assumed management roles in their firms, or trained managers who have chosen to apply their skills in design firms. It is also to be hoped that it may find its way into the education of the increasing number of student engineers and architects who are wisely choosing to add MBA degrees to their preparation for practice.

There is another audience for this book that I especially want to recognize. This is the large number of design professionals who may read this in order to decide that they do *not* want to add management to the other functions they presently perform. Managing is neither an easy nor enjoyable task for all those who choose to practice. Many skilled and dedicated practitioners will be far better engineers and architects if they learn how to let others manage for them.

This book will have accomplished its purpose if it helps all of these readers become better at what they and their organizations must continue to do best—provide professional design service for clients.

WELD COXE

Philadelphia, Pennsylvania
August 1980

ACKNOWLEDGMENTS

This book would not be in your hands without the following special contributions:

C. Van R. Bogert, Jr., George Borkovich, Joseph Chrobak, Edward L. Crow, Thomas Harack, Nina F. Hartung, Hugh M. Hochberg, Louis Marines, Jack McNichol, Robert F. Mattox, Carol McConochie, Martin C. P. McElroy, Henry W. Schirmer, Frank A. Stasiowski, David Vachon, and others who, as past and present colleagues in the consulting work at The Coxe Group, management consultants, have shared much of the experience and provided many of the insights that are documented here.

Peter A. Piven, ditto, and for his additional assistance as contributing author to Chapter 8, "Managing the Numbers."

N. Boyce Appel, ditto, and for his enlightenment to and review of the material of Chapter 7, "Managing Human Resources."

William S. Findlay, Neil Harper, and Michael R. Hough for reading portions of the manuscript in draft and providing helpful corrections and comments.

Mary Chapman Hayden, ditto, and for so many helpful dialogues and support at important times and places.

Robin J. Tufts for patiently administering the production of the manuscript.

The waterfronts of Bequia, W.I., and Block Island, R.I., and a boat named Toge for the stimulating environments where most of the original writing was done.

And most especially the many, many individual architects and engineers who, as clients of The Coxe Group over 14 years, allowed me to learn so much at their expense. Whatever value this book may provide to others is, in the final analysis, the return on their investment.

W.C.

CONTENTS

FIVE   HAVING THE ANSWERS IS NOT NECESSARILY
THE ANSWER

APPENDIXES

Most management structures in design firms are on the cutting edge of mayhem all the time. It ain't like it's written in the text book.

Joseph C. Roher, General Manager
Gruzen and Partners

ONE

WHAT IT'S ALL ABOUT

Chapter 1
THE BOTTOM LINE
IS NOT
THE BOTTOM LINE

"Solving technical problems is the easiest thing to do in a consulting practice. Its the business aspects of running the firm that give professionals the most trouble."

Arnold Olitt, P.E.
Founding Partner
Woodward-Clyde, Consultants

3

M anaging design practice is different from managing a business. The management of design practice embraces aspects of capability assessment, quality control, marketing planning, organization structure, human resources development, financial management, organization transition, and many others. Some might say that this book will accomplish its purpose if it can just provide the answers to all these concerns. But the principal architect or engineer who has been striving to manage a practice for a few years and who has been to a few seminars or read some books on general business management knows that successful practice management is not a matter of answers alone. To understand why this is so, one must accept that design practice operates under some special rules that derive from the nature of the creative process.

One of these factors is the task orientation of the professional service firm. Typically, the first management experience of architects and engineers is on a single project. Either it is the first project experience of young design professionals in an established firm or it is the first job of a new firm. Either way, the goal is to execute the project for the client, and the degree to which the management requirements of that task are successfully handled usually determines whether the individuals will get a commission to design another project.

If they do, more often than not the principals replicate the management pattern that was successful on the original project, and the practice evolves into an organization of projects. Many firms level off at this stage of evolution and exist for years in what is really a project organization model. The client's needs are always seen as paramount; the reward is in the design result and/or client satisfaction; and the impact of all this on personal life style, up-and-down workloads, staff growth and development or financial performance—whether good or bad—is seen as inevitable.

Such firms become skilled at *project* management, and either fail to recognize or choose to ignore the distinctions between this model and *practice* management. So long as there are so many clients stating problems and asking for help it is very easy to focus on the result or task, rather than the process.

Frequently, those who are seen—and see themselves—as the most successful in a design firm are those who are most task oriented. The best managers, on the other hand, are process oriented—persons who get their kicks from oiling the gears of the organization so that it, rather than they, accomplishes the task. This factor often explains why the strong design professional, who is accustomed to making successful project decisions on a day-to-day basis, is so frustrated when the decisions he or she imposes on the organization don't produce similar results.

Not until the day comes when the practice is seen as having a life of its own, above and beyond that of its clients, is the firm ready for organization management. From that day forward there will be principals in the firm who understand that the needs of the organization will from time to time be more important than the needs of any one client, and they will begin managing the practice to achieve its own goals—as well as serve clients.

Another factor that separates design firm management from business management is the decision-making process itself. Psychologists are beginning to confirm that the human brain has a finite capacity for the number of decisions it can make at any one time—just like a computer memory has a capacity for the number of bytes it can process at once. The act of creative design is probably the most decision-consuming process of man, and thus it is not surprising that many designers go home at night and say to their spouses: "You decide what we are going to do this evening—I can't make another decision today." Unfortunately, for many design organizations, the principal designers often use up their decision-making capacity long before they go home, and especially when decisions are needed on whether to select this or that insurance program (or a new piece of office equipment); or to give staff members thoughtful performance feedback; or to change a contract form to get better fees. Seeing decisions on such matters as irritations and constantly putting them off, or making them in haste, is a symptom of overload. The decision overload factor tends to affect architects more severely than engineers, because of the greater demands of the architectural design process, which may explain why, on the whole, architectural firms are generally less managed than engineering firms.

The primary factor that separates management of design practice from management of a business is the fact that the professional's bottom line is not the same as the businessman's bottom line. The businessman is trained to measure the success of management in chiefly *quantitative* terms—usually units of money, or output, or the like. In contrast, the bottom line of the creative professional is most often *qualitative*— measured in terms of the professional's ultimate judgment about whether

the output of the organization is as good as it can be. This single distinction is the most common reason why the many books and courses about
business management don't ring quite true to the design professional.

For example, the *quantitative* manager will be inclined to deal with
overruns in design budgets by imposing a design freeze as soon as the time
allocation for design is used up. The *qualitative* manager, on the other
hand, will frequently tolerate the overrun and justify it on the basis that
it produced a better solution. Similarly, the *quantitative* manager will
likely accept work in lean times or reject work in busy times simply on
the basis of its contribution to volume and profit objectives. The qualitative manager in such cases will frequently select work to pursue solely on
the basis of its professional interest, and may allow the firm to suffer
severe ups and downs as a consequence. In the final analysis, the *quantitative* manager will usually measure a life's work by the size of the estate left
behind; the *qualitative* manager's measurement will be in terms of the
work accomplished and its impact on the society/profession left behind.

Business schools teach modern managers to measure organization
performance in *quantitative* terms because these criteria can be established
objectively and compared analytically. To date there has been very little
attention paid to teaching managers how to measure performance in
qualitative terms in *qualitative* organizations.

The combination of these factors—the qualitative bottom line; the
task rather than process orientation; and the frequent decision
overload—by no means justify a lack of management in a design firm.
Rather, they define an environment in which conventional management
wisdom must be applied with special understanding. Otherwise, the very
strengths of the creative design process will be thwarted by the management process.

The business of architectural and engineering practice is design.
The role of management in architectural and engineering practice is to
provide an environment in which design can flourish. That is the bottom
line of this book.

Chapter 2

"PASSAGES" OF DESIGN FIRMS

The first step in managing any organization is to know its goals. And before goal setting can begin, it is essential to know where you are starting from.

In this respect, firm managers are no different from the navigators on a sailing ship. If the ship does not have a destination, it will merely follow the winds—and arrive wherever they take it. On the other hand, if the crew knows they want to get to point B on the map, it is easy to know how to sail day-to-day, regardless of the winds—provided that you know your current position. A ship headed for point B cannot be navigated if no one aboard knows whether it is north, south, east, or west of that objective. To fix the present position in a design firm, it is necessary to make realistic assessments of your professional capabilities, your organization resources, and your present "passage" in the evolution process.

The term "passage" is used here in the same context as Gail Sheehy's book of the same title,* which describes the predictable patterns of human behavior at different ages in maturity. Design organizations go through similar passages with almost anthropological certainty. Some examples:

PASSAGE 1: THE ONE-PERSON PRACTICE PASSAGE

This might be subtitled "Why there are so many five-person design firms." For design firms with a single principal, the first passage generally occurs when the staff grows to seven or nine, and the principal is involved in getting all the work, serving as the project manager and designer on that work, and also trying to operate all the business and personnel aspects of the firm.

Symptoms: A 60 or 70 hour workweek for the principal who finds that this is still not enough time to do all the things that need to be done; a feeling that the principal is always putting out fires and never has enough time for his or her priorities; staff frustration because of difficulty in getting decisions from the principal; high turnover among the staff the principal most wants to keep; and clients who are originally very pleased with the personal attention of the principal, but gradually have to prod to

Passages by Gail Sheehy, E. P. Dutton, 1976.

8

get action rather than relying on the architect or engineer to lead the project.

Problem: A firm at this passage has outgrown the ability of one principal to be all things to all the problems. Once in discussing this phenomenon an architect observed; "Now I understand what my father meant. He was a carpenter, and they have a rule: The day the carpenter hires his fourth helper, he must lay down his own tools."

This means that there is a practical numerical limit to the number of people who can be managed effectively by someone who is holding sole responsibility for everything those people do. For carpenters—and for architects and engineers—that practical limit is about five people.

Solutions: There are only two options open when this passage occurs. One is to hold the practice to four or five people and enjoy the fruits of being a "renaissance person"—the classic "whole architect" or "whole engineer" who is a master of all aspects of the discipline—design, technology, construction, and client service. There is nothing wrong—and there are many rewards—in being a renaissance architect or engineer today, provided you are willing to accept the practical limitations on the amount and size of work you can do and the kind of organization you will have as a consequence. Any other course—that is, a larger organization or larger work—requires that the principal make hard choices of delegation and become less than "whole." Common solutions are to delegate the outside, or field work, or to delegate (or ignore) some of the organization management considerations, or to delegate some of the technical responsibility for specifications, working drawings, and so on. This often means appointing a job captain to pick up and take over projects at a certain stage. Or the principals who are self-analytical enough to know their own limitations may even delegate design! But not everyone wants to delegate, and it is that choice that ultimately determines the management complexion—and future size—of the firm.

Common Variations of This Passage

The numerical rule applies in multiprincipal firms as well. If there are two partners, each of whom is trying to be a "whole" professional, the management crunch will occur when the total staff reaches 10 to 15. If there are three partners, it will occur between 15 and 20 staff, and so on.

As the number of partners grows, an affiliated phenomenon often appears known as: "This is Not One Firm—It Is Really Four Practices Sharing a Common Address." The consequences of this organization pattern, if not obvious, are discussed further in Chapter 4.

PASSAGE 2: THE "WHY-DOES-EVERYONE-HAVE-TO-MAKE-EVERY-DECISION?" PASSAGE

This passage normally occurs in multiprincipal firms where there is division of technical roles when the staff size grows to 15 to 20. It generally doesn't matter how many partners there are, if we assume that the organization is operating as a firm, with each of the principals or key people having some client responsibility as well as a delegated role in an area such as design, production, or field observation.

Symptoms: Growing unbalance of workload among the principals—one bringing in much more of the work than another; increasing feelings that some principals are pulling more of the oars than others; neglect of business affairs, and housekeeping; and; "Nobody can make a decision around here unless we have a committee meeting."

Problem: This organization is beginning to outgrow the ability of all the leaders to juggle many different balls in the air at the same time. With each leader carrying responsibility for several clients who can call at any hour and get prime attention, plus responsibility for getting new work, plus some voice in overall organization decision making, there are just too many things going on for everyone to be involved in the organization itself. But nobody wants to be the first to give up contact with clients and projects.

Solution: This firm can stop growing where it is and work within the practical limits of a size that it sets for itself. Or, someone in this firm will have to accept a prime-time management role and become disengaged from primary client/project responsibility. In order for this firm to pass through this passage and continue to grow, someone at the top echelon must be spending full time tending to the organization's priorities—such as production scheduling, personnel, operations and financial control—and not be tugged at whenever a client calls. This means that all the other principals must be prepared to yield some of their authority to a manager with authority to act in certain areas without calling a meeting of the partnership or the board of directors.

PASSAGE 3: THE "JOE-HAS-GOT-TO-STOP-TRYING-TO-DESIGN-EVERY-PROJECT-IN-THE-OFFICE" PASSAGE

Depending on whether this firm is doing small projects or very large projects, this phenomenon can occur anywhere in evolution from a staff of 10 to maybe 100 or more.

Symptoms: Difficulty in meeting schedules, often a growing unprofitability, especially during the design phase when budgets are never maintained; and so on.

Problem: Pride of authorship is the single most pervasive motivation that compels architects and engineers to put up with the trials of professional design practice. Some firms let every project team have a crack at design. But others focus design responsibility in a single designer—or a single design stream. (Firms with two or more strong design streams often find that there is so much conflict about who will design which job that the firm eventually splits.) However, organizations with a single design stream eventually reach the limit of that designer to personally control all the work.

Solutions: Again, this firm can decide to stop growing, and knuckle under to the designer who has to have his or her personal imprint on every job. Or, the designer in charge can back off to a "quality control" role and oversee the work of other designers, without personally controlling all of it. For some designers this shift is relatively easy. For others it is impossible. For most, it is painful, slow to be implemented, and can result in severe constipation within the organization until it is cured.

PASSAGE 4: THE "HOW-COME-IT'S-NOT-WORKING-LIKE-IT-USED-TO" PASSAGE

This phase occurs in firms of all sizes shortly after the retirement of the founder(s).

Symptoms: Erosion of the original client base; difficulty in obtaining new clients; gradual shrinking of the staff, usually with the loss of the younger talent first, leaving an ever older average age among those remaining.

Problem: This is a classic "Second Team Syndrome." The strong founder(s) (or previous leaders) surrounded themselves with very qualified support professionals, but did not promote or welcome to key positions persons as strong as themselves. Anyone with such ambitions long ago left the firm, and when control was passed it was placed in the hands of the dedicated and loyal second-level people who had stayed on in the shadow of the previous stars. They waited long and expectantly for the chance to take over, never realizing that their very patience may have signaled the absence of the sparks that are necessary to lead the firm as it was led before.

Solutions: The new principals can throttle back, and live off what is left of the former client base until they, too, are ready to retire. But the price will be high, as the declining workload fails to cover the high overhead of the past, and the firm begins to lose money and run up high debts. Then, if they are lucky, they can sell out to a larger, national firm that believes (often wrongly) there is some good will value in the reputation of the past that will help the buyer capture the local market. Or, if the second generation can swallow their pride, they can bring in strong younger blood and give them the reins so that they of the second team can go back to doing just exactly what they have always done best.

PASSAGE 5: THE "WHAT'S-GOING-TO-HAPPEN-WHEN-I'M-GONE?" PASSAGE

This passage could be subtitled: "I am (we are) nearing 60 and I (we) don't see what's going to happen next."

Symptoms: Everyone at the top is over 55 and anyone with potential is under 30; the firm has lost a lot of good people over the years who are now among its major competitors; the organization is beginning to lose old and loyal clients to younger firms.

Problem: The principals of this firm enjoyed having it all to themselves too long, and have not made provision for organization transition. This might be called the "final" passage in organization maturity. This passage can be reached by organizations of any size and is solely a factor of the age of the principal(s).

Solutions: Wait for the day when the last job is finished, collect the receivables, lay off the staff, turn the key in the door, and go off to retirement—if you have any money left and your ego can stand it. The only alternative is to start handing over authority, responsibility, and a big piece of the action to bright young people long before you think they are ready—somewhere in their mid-30's when they are at or near the same age as the founders were when they started. Then be prepared to watch them go through all the foregoing passages and make the same mistakes as they learn—they won't listen to you if you tell them anyway. But if you do succeed in handing over real control to such a group, the firm will have continuity, and the senior principals can expect to recover their equity and receive handsome deferred compensation as "consultants" to the firm well beyond normal retirement age.

Enough examples? There are numerous other passages, with perhaps as many variations as there are design firms. The point is that firms must be realistic about where they are when they start the management process.

DETERMINING YOUR OWN PASSAGE

What it takes to know where you are is the ability to make a realistic self-assessment of the organization. One way to do this is to list the firm's strengths and weaknesses in a matrix that might look like Table 1.

If the process of making such an assessment is done formally, it is best to have each principal fill out the matrix before comparing notes as a group. Organizations with an open internal system can often benefit by involving the staff in the process. In a small firm this might mean having every employee list his or her perception of the strengths and weaknesses. In larger firms it is usually more practical to appoint one or more small (three members is plenty) task groups to sample the staff assessment on a group or department basis and present a consolidated or consensus report to management. (Caution: if you are going to involve staff in such a process, read Chapter 7 before asking your employees questions to which you might not want to hear the answers.)

Another group that may be very helpful in making a self-assessment is the firm's clients. Many firms don't consider conducting an "image" study unless they think they are in trouble, and then they usually seek an outside consultant to do the study for them. In fact, the best time to

Table 1   Self-Assessment Inventory

Where We Are Now	Our Strengths	Our Weaknesses
Professionally: in capability and services		
Externally: in terms of our market and competition		
Internally: in terms of our human and organization resources		
Personally: in terms of our individual life forces and goals		

check your image with your clients may be just when everything seems to be fine. A firm's clients are often its best friends, and they are usually very pleased to be asked to participate in a process intended to strengthen the firm. The best way to involve your clients is not through a third party or mailed questionnaire, but directly, face-to-face. Ask your client to lunch, tell him or her that you are beginning a goal-setting process for the firm and that the first step is to make a realistic assessment of your present strengths and weaknesses. Ask the client to tell you candidly:

- What are we best at?
- What could we be better at?
- What, if anything, are we not doing or offering that might be useful to the client if we did?
- How does the client see our strengths and weaknesses in relation to what the client may know about our competition?

People like nothing better than to be asked for advice. Involving your clients in your self-assessment can produce directly valuable input, and it can have real marketing benefits in cementing a client relationship. A client who feels he or she has made a contribution to your future is very likely to want to stay around to see how it comes out.

Although the process of self-assessment is fairly straightforward, arriving at realistic conclusions isn't always easy. One of the characteristics of many successful design professionals—especially architects—is a strong ego. While this may be a strength in leading clients to accept innovative design solutions on projects, it can often be a liability when applied to the designer's own firm. Persons with strong egos often have difficulty being realistic about their own strengths and weaknesses—especially in front of others, even their partners. In design organizations, it is important to acknowledge that the personal styles of the individuals at the head of the firm will have everything to do with how that firm can be managed. Beginning with self-assessment, and all through the management process, the pivotal issue is who will make the decisions.

Since most professional firms are closely held, the managing group is usually the ownership group. In small partnerships there is a choice between following the direction of a single leader in such matters or working by consensus. In larger organizations, particularly the corporately organized engineering firms where ownership is spread among many employees, the question of who makes the navigating decisions can be more complicated, involving boards of directors and officers. Frequently, a key founder will retain the presumed power to make or veto certain key decisions—such as goals—long after the founder's ownership has been diluted.

For now, the point to be made is that without an agreement about who has the right to decide, there will be no decisions. The first "passage" toward successful management of a design firm is deciding who will decide the goals.

TWO
GETTING ORGANIZED

Chapter 3
WHERE IS THE PRACTICE GOING?

"Firms that don't plan, manage or determine their destiny, won't have one."

George L. Schrohe
President
Management Design

B ecause of their different bottom lines, professional firms often have difficulty in setting clear goals.

Organizations with a quantitative bottom line can usually set very concrete goals—for example, to realize a specific return or investment; to maintain a specified market share; to grow at x % per year.

On the other hand, architects or engineers who have a qualitative bottom line tend to state goals more in terms of ideals: to do "good" work; to build a "better" environment. There is certainly nothing wrong with aspiring to "motherhood" ideals, but the difficult part comes when you try to define such a goal. It is impossible to manage a course toward a goal you cannot define.

To use an earlier analogy, the navigator who sets a course for "London" has a much clearer management task than the navigator who wants to sail to a "bright new world."

In terms of organization direction, it is necessary to understand the difference between goals, objectives, strategies, and tactics.

- Goals, as used in this book, are the desired result—such as world peace.
- Objectives, in this context, are the milestones en route to that goal—end the conflict in the Middle East, for example.
- Strategies, are the means to the objectives—e.g. get some of the adversaries talking.
- Tactics are the step-by-step actions taken to carry out the strategy—such as inviting two of the adversaries to Camp David.

At all levels on this ladder, the distinction between a manageable goal or objective and an unmanageable one is whether the end result is measurable. Thus the goal:

"We want to be the best design firm in Indiana"

is difficult to work toward, because there are likely to be many different measurements of "best." A more manageable goal statement might be:

"We want to be recognized for the quality of our design work"

Such a goal could be measured in these terms:

"We want our work to be published at least ____ times a year in ____ magazine."

"We want to receive design awards in at least two out of every three annual awards programs of the state (ACEC) (AIA), etc."

"We want our clients to talk about us as an 'award winning' or 'innovative' firm."

Sometimes the goal can be measured in terms of the objective. For example, the goal

"We want to become a multidiscipline firm"

could be translated into the first objective:

"We will open an Interiors Department within one year"

launched with the strategy:

"We will begin by recruiting an experienced interior designer to head the department"

and implemented by this tactical management step:

"Bill has the responsibility to locate the interior designer and is authorized to agree to compensation up to $ ____ ." (Or it could say: "Bill is authorized to search for at least two qualified candidates, and to present them to the full partnership for interviews and final decision.")

In practical terms, for architects and engineers, goals should state what you want your practice to be. There is nothing wrong with idealistic goals provided you know how you will measure the results. And there is also nothing wrong with concrete, quantitative goals for a professional firm (e.g. "We want to be the largest civil engineering firm in town") provided you have a handle on what you must be qualitatively—in terms of the quality of service you render your clients—in order to achieve the quantitative goals.

Whatever the goals of the practice, once defined they must be translated into objectives for a number of very specific aspects of practice. For example:

Firm Capability(ies):   What disciplines, expertise, and services will we offer?

Markets: Whom will we seek to serve? How far will we travel?

Firm Size: How large a staff will we need?

Volume: How much work will we need to support this organization?

Financial: What must we put up to make it happen? What do we expect in return?*

Personal Goals of the Decision Group: What will each of us contribute through our roles and what does each of us want in return?

Some of these goal/objective areas are discussed more fully in the succeeding chapters that deal with managing individual aspects of practice. But don't wait to set goals until you know how to manage them. You have a right first to aspire to whatever you really want to be.

In practice, the area of personal goals, listed last above, should be the starting place for goal setting in a professional design firm. The common business management theory that sets organization goals ahead of personal goals derives from the business assumption of stockholder ownership, with managers as caretakers of someone else's investment. (It further follows that since this investment is usually financial, the goals are financial). This is not so in most professional firms. By usual definition—and many state laws—a professional firm is controlled by those in its active management, and thus their personal and professional goals are inseparable from the organization goals.

When the managers of an absentee-owned business get together to discuss sales goals, if Bill doesn't want to work as hard as the goals require, he can usually be replaced by someone who will agree to try. Conversely, when the partners in an engineering or architectural firm get

---

*It is important to note that a major difference between a business and a professional service firm is the degree to which "making money" is a goal of the proprietors. There is a rampant myth in American business culture that the reason behind everything is the goal of making money. Certainly some organizations are trying hard to do this. But in professional design firms, the author's observation is that the making of money over the long term occurs only as a by-product of giving good service. A client who perceives that your first goal is to line your own pockets will not stay a client long.

together and Bill is one of those partners in the room, it is not a question of what he *ought to do* for the firm. Rather it is a matter of what Bill, in terms of his personal and professional goals, *will do* that sets the course of the organization.

Some design firm partners may say, "We want the firm to grow, but we don't personally want to work that hard; let's hire the talent to do it for us." Well and good if you can manage it, but generally as soon as that talent finds out the firm's success depends more on their efforts than on yours, they will demand to be your partners, or they will become your competitors. This is why so few of the engineering and architectural firms that were bought out by businesses in the late 1960s have remained successful. If the best professional talents in an organization don't control their own destiny, they quickly leave to go into practice for themselves—where they can set their own goals.

Another personal factor that affects professional firm goals is risk. It has long been an axiom that the success of any new business is proportionate to the risk the founders are willing to take. This, for example, is why wise bankers require personal guarantees on real estate loans— because they know the entrepreneurs will work harder if their shirts are at stake. It is less recognized that, at least until recently, most practicing architects and engineers have come from the lower risk-taking cross section of our society. The design professions have attracted individuals of principle, dedication, and ideals, but these are not always qualities found in high risk takers. This behavioral profile is demonstrated in practice in such ways as the degree to which a design firm will challenge and lead its clients vs. doing what it is told to do, and in the kind of lease the partners will sign for office space. (It is interesting to observe how many architects have office space inferior to that which they would consider designing for any client.)

The point to be made about the risk factor when setting goals is simply to recognize it. If the decision group in a practice is not risk oriented, they will probably set goals that require limited personal exposure—both financially and professionally—and be comfortable with the results. It is when one partner or a group of partners want to take substantially different risks that things get sticky.

The process of goal setting may founder at such points if it is not well managed. The only valid goals for a design practice are those that are fully integrated with the personal goals and styles of those who set them. Thus goal setting must begin with free and open communication among the goal setters. Unstated differences or open conflicts in the group that are not managed will lead either to unrealistic goals (because not everyone is committed) or to no goals at all.

Thus the process through which goals are set is the most important management process in a design firm. It should be done formally, in an atmosphere removed from day-to-day pressures. It must be given enough time.

In practice, the best format for goal setting is for the decision group to meet in a retreat environment—away from the office and, if possible, away overnight so the participants will not be distracted by at-home concerns each evening. The length of time required is a factor of past experience at goal-setting retreats, and the number of participants. If goal setting is to be truly participative, each person needs a certain amount of "air time" to have their point of view heard. As a general rule, groups of five or fewer members may have a productive retreat in two days. Add an additional day for every three to five additional participants.

Often the most effective way to make such a retreat productive is to hire a behavioral facilitator trained in group process. The facilitator is not there to help set goals, but to observe the communication process in the group and see that differences and conflicts are brought to the surface and effectively managed. Also, the presence of a third party can help prevent deterioration of the agenda into a staff meeting; domination by one or another participant; or acceptance of inconclusive (nonmeasurable) objectives.

If you feel you must conduct the retreat yourself, keep in mind a few management processes that can help get things off on the right track.

One helpful device is to have each person, at the outset of the retreat, complete in writing the following statements:

1   The best thing(s) that could happen at this retreat, for me personally, would be ____.
2   The worst thing(s) that could happen at this retreat, for me personally, would be ____.

These statements should be prepared privately, then posted on a wall, read by all, and discussed to make certain that each person's starting points are understood.

It is sometimes helpful at this point to ask each participant to estimate on a scale of 0 to 10 the probability for a successful outcome of the retreat. These probability forecasts can be repeated once or twice a day throughout the retreat as a means of learning how the different participants are feeling about the ongoing process.

Another process device that can be helpful in integrating personal goals with goals and roles in the organization is to ask each participant to list personal wants by completing the following statements:

- For me to be more effective in my role, I would like from the organization *more:* _____.
- For me to be more effective in my role I would like from the organization *less:* _____.
- For me to continue to be effective in my role, I would like from the organization the *same:* _____.

As before, each person should first prepare answers privately. Then the individual answers can be consolidated (preferably on large newsprint or a blackboard) in a master list grouped by what the individuals want "more of," "less of," and the "same as" from the organization. As the retreat discussion focuses on how to achieve these, considerable progress can be made toward realistic goals.

The output from the goal-setting process, however it is conducted, should be a written list of goals, and objectives, plus specific assignments of responsibility with due dates by which individuals will prepare detailed strategies for implementation.

How far ahead can you plan? This is a constant dilemma in design firms. Since they are service organizations, much of their destiny is shaped by the needs of the clients they serve. In recent years, the rate of social, economic, and technological changes that affect design firms has made it very difficult to plan in any detail more than three to five years ahead. But some of the larger engineering firms have been experimenting with much longer range goal setting—as far ahead as 15 and 20 years. Only time will tell how practical this may be.

Basically, it is best to express goals in two time frames:

Long-Range Goals: What we want the practice to be in three to five years.

Short-Range Goals: What we want the practice to be one year from now, as a step toward long-range goals.

When a professional practice has its goals documented clearly, it is already well on the way to being managed. With the destination of the practice set, day-to-day management can go to work monitoring the course. The chapters that follow are intended to provide some help along these routes.

Chapter 4

CHOOSING ORGANIZATION STRUCTURE

Selecting an organization structure is the first—and often the single most important—management choice to be made in implementating goals. The structure of a design firm determines how it will serve its clients, and what kind of roles by principals and staff will be needed to provide that service.

Selecting the right organization structure for a design practice involves considerations of client management; design process; and organization control. Each factor needs to be considered for its own implications and they often conflict with one another. The final organization structure must be a parity of all three.

CLIENT MANAGEMENT CONSIDERATIONS

There can be no design practice without a client, and the client must be an integral part of every design firm's organization structure. At the project level, this is usually accomplished in one of two ways.

In Figure 1 a principal takes charge of managing the client and the project and serves as the link between the client and the firm for the life of the job. This is the most common pattern in small and medium size firms.

The variation shown in Figure 2 is common in larger firms where the number of projects outgrows the number of principals. Each project is then delegated to a staff or project manager who provides continuity to the client for the life of the project.

Both structures are basically strong project manager formats, with the difference being whether or not the manager is a principal. Both work well once the client link with the project manager is adequately cemented. In practice, however, cementing that link is not always easy, and as a consequence there are many variations in structure that creep into firms because of the nature of the professional service process. These can seriously weaken the organization if not effectively managed.

Consider the client management structure shown in Figure 3. This is a project where the client established his or her initial relationship with the principal who marketed the job. That principal does not want to be involved in executing the project and therefore intends to hand the technical work to another principal or department head. This is fine in concept, except that in this case the client doesn't accept a complete handoff and keeps coming back to the marketing principal for some of

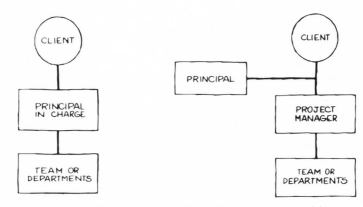

Figure 1   Principal In Charge.   **Figure 2**   Strong Project Manager.

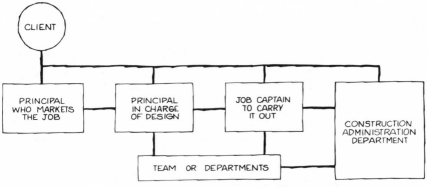

Figure 3   Many (or No One) In Charge.

the job communication. As the project continues, the principal in charge of design finishes the concepts and wants to hand the execution to a job captain so he or she can go on to other work. When the job goes into the field, another handoff is supposed to occur as the job captain, usually a superior "inside" person, turns over day-to-day contact to an "outside" specialist. In this format, is it any wonder the marketing principal can never be extracted from the job?

Variations of the case shown in Figure 3 take place in virtually every design firm every day. The logic from the architect's or engineer's point of view is obvious: each person in the organization concentrates on what they do best, and the project is passed along the firm's "assembly line" until it is done.

The difficulty is that while assembly lines may be excellent organizations on which to build automobiles, the client for that automobile doesn't enter the auto company's organization picture until the product is finished. On the other hand, a professional service firm is always juggling a dichotomy: part of its product is the service to the client and part of its product is the project result. Whereas some professional firms may be able to deal in an assembly line fashion, most clients don't like it at all. They engage a professional to design their project and they want/expect that professional to take them by the hand and lead them through the maze until the project is finished. This is an essential ingredient of the professional process. If the client wanted an assembly line process, the client would buy stock-plan structures.

Thus the choice of organization structure in a professional firm has considerable influence on the type of clients who are comfortable in giving their work to that firm—or vice versa.

To choose an effective structure, it is first necessary to understand the difference between client management and project management. The starting point in professional service is managing the client. Doing this effectively takes as much time and attention as the client requires. For example, a client who hires an engineer and then delegates the project in the client's organization will generally accept delegation within the engineer's organization. But a client who wants to be intimately involved in every aspect of the design of the project will demand that the principal professional be equally involved in every aspect of that project.

As a rule of thumb, the client will insist on as much principal attention from the architect's or engineer's organization as the client will give to the project in his or her organization. This fundamental consideration of professional relationships explains why most private residential architecture is done by small design firms, and why most governmental engineering is done by larger, more bureaucratically organized engineering firms.

DESIGN PROCESS CONSIDERATIONS

From a management standpoint, the choice of a structure for the design process is a matter of communication and coordination. Most architectural and engineering work today involves multiple disciplines and multiple functions, and the role of management in the design process is to keep projects moving among these functions and disciplines in an efficient and effective sequence.

There are two primary variations.

Figure 4 illustrates a departmentalized structure where each major function (or discipline) of the design process is separately managed. The department head is responsible for both the function and the staff necessary to perform that function. Such a format usually provides tight, efficient control of each major segment of the design process and can accommodate various sizes of projects simultaneously within a department. Its limitations lie in coordinating and scheduling functions, and in the need to categorize staff within single functions, whereas many design professionals prefer a broader role in projects.

Figure 5 illustrates the so-called team approach structure, where a group of professionals, assembled for a specific project, perform all the functions required to execute it. Such a format focuses the team's attention on all aspects of the project or projects at hand, thus fostering close coordination. The format appeals to staff professionals with broader interest in the design process. The limitations of this format come in the

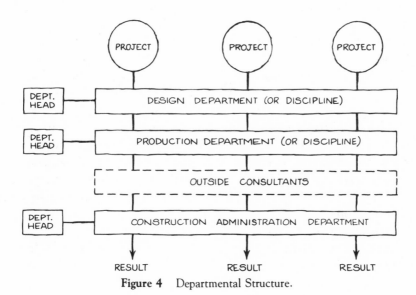

Figure 4   Departmental Structure.

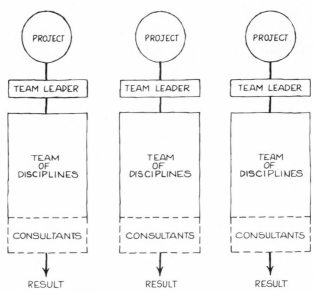

Figure 5   Project Team Structure.

difficulty in encouraging firmwide standards for all teams; in the relatively inflexibility of the teams to adapt to different-sized projects and/or
schedule interruptions; and in personnel management, since the team
leader tends to be task oriented and looks to someone else in the firm to
provide human resources to the team. In practice, the team approach
works best on larger projects in large firms. In smaller firms (or with
smaller projects in a large firm) the team becomes a studio of people who
work together as a team on a variety of simultaneous projects.

The team studio approach is often costlier to operate because of the
difficulty or reassigning people between teams during short-term down
periods. On the other hand, the departmentalized approach tends not to
train from within the kind of staff needed for multifunction project
management and firm management roles. In the long run the two costs
may almost offset each other.

The choice of departmental vs. team approach is best made based on
the format in which the specific people work best. This can often lead to
hybrid structures, such as those shown in Figures 6 and 7.

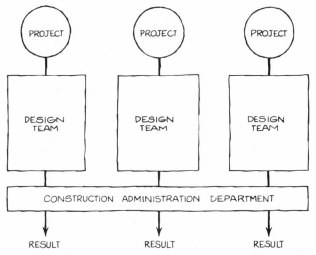

Figure 6 Hybrid Structure.

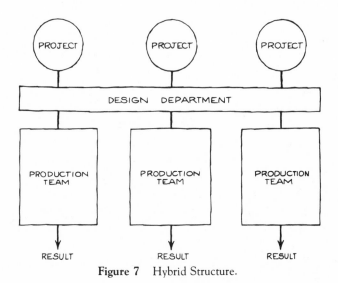

Figure 7 Hybrid Structure.

33

ORGANIZATION CONTROL CONSIDERATIONS

At the management center of every organization a number of functions must be performed to control the organization's progress en route to its goals. There are two approaches to fulfilling these functions, and it is important to understand their definition.

> *Leadership:* The function of setting goals for where the firm will go and of establishing the major policies that will define the route to be taken to get there. Leadership can be vested in a strong individual or in a group of partners or directors. At the bottom line, the leadership sets the tone of the firm.
>
> *Management:* The function of helping people steer the course set by a leader or group of owners. In design practice it involves managing the marketing to find the kind of clients the firm wants; managing the human resources to see that the necessary staff is attracted to do the work; and managing the assignments, schedules, budgets, and other factors that are necessary to make it all happen in a productive way.

There are several ways (styles) in which management can be performed. Management can be provided in a directive, autocratic manner, which is frequently the case when the leader and manager are one and the same. Or management can be provided in a facilitative manner, with the Manager being an agent of the leadership and entrusted with the role of seeing that the functions are performed by and throughout the organization.

The choice of management approach is often a function of the style of the leader(s). In small design organizations one person frequently wears all the hats. In group practices the management functions are frequently divided, and several people wear dual hats as part-time organization manager and part-time functional/discipline/client manager. In terms of organization structure, however, the number of people involved in management is not as important as their management style. Directive management control has implications on the organization structure that are very different from those of facilitative management.

Generally, when people think of organization structures they tend to visualize the pyramidal format that is typical of organizations designed for hierarchical decision making. See Figure 8, for example.

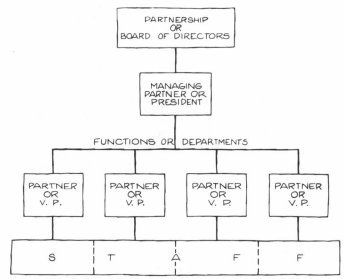

Figure 8   Typical Business Organization Heirarchy.

While this organization pattern is sufficient for many business organizations, it is difficult for professional practice because it does not
make clear where the client fits. Since the purpose of a structure is to
define the routes of management control, a design firm structure that
does not include the client defines only the internal management
process—and this is only a small portion of the management that must go
on in design practice.

To include the client in a design practice structure requires a format
such as that shown in Figure 9.

What is missing from Figure 9 is an illustration of how the organization itself is managed. Nevertheless, many design firms—especially
partnerships—operate very much like this and simply omit a structure for
management. In its place a series of partnership/staff meetings serve the
management function. This is inefficient at best, and usually leads to
lowest-common-denominator decision making and a lot of individual
autonomy at the expense of organization strength.

There are two basic options to include management into the format
in Figure 9, and the choice is defined by whether the control is to be
directive or facilitative.

Figure 10 illustrates a strongly directive management, where deci-

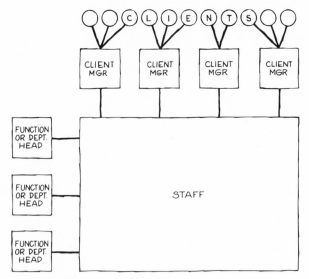

Figure 9   Typical Service Organization Matrix.

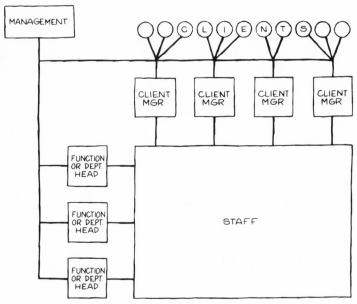

Figure 10   Directed Organization Structure.

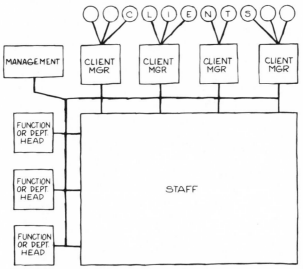

Figure 11   Managed Organization Structure.

sions about product, marketing, personnel, and so on are decided at the top and fed down into the organization. This most closely parallels the pyramidal concept in Figure 8. The last word in the organization is closely held, clients know it, and most work comes in through or because of the principal manager. The strength of this structure is the clear, quick format for decisions, and the ability to deliver a strong, consistent quality of service. Its primary limitation is the physical inability of a single control source to do it all. Another limitation is the frequent difficulty of autocratic management to retain good talent in a design practice. The format works best in smaller organizations.

An alternative approach is that given in Figure 11. In this format the management functions are more facilitative and less autocratic. Management's role here is to coordinate and provide support and encouragement for a group of unit leaders, rather than to tell everyone autocratically what to do. Its strengths are in the way the collaborative format supports the multidiscipline, multifunction nature of today's practice and in its ability to grow, since the burdens of management are shared by a group. It also fosters growth of future leaders from within. The independence that it allows individuals, however, can lead to problems in maintaining a consistent organization process. There is also a very real shortage of management-inclined design professionals who want to fill the central management role (see Chapter 12).

Architects and engineers are trained to control most of their decisions themselves, rather than manage a decision process involving others. It is for this reason probably more than any other that so many design professionals practice in small organizations where they can do it all themselves. There is absolutely nothing wrong with this approach to practice, so long as it is a choice willingly made in the light of the implications and consequences.

In the end, the best structure is the one that is most effective for the people involved. Since no two people are alike, there is no reason why two structures must be alike. Don't copy someone else's structure just because it works for them. Find what works for you, while fulfilling the considerations of client management, design process, and organization control, and you will have the foundation for good practice.

The chapters that follow discuss the management functions of all practice, whether large or small. The purpose of the structure, as already discussed, is to provide the format in which those functions will be performed.

THREE
MAKING
IT WORK

Chapter 5

MANAGING PROFESSIONAL PERFORMANCE

"The whole business about design architects and production architects is horseshit!"

Eugene E. Aubry
Partner
Morris/Aubry Associates

41

The most important element of design practice is the nature and quality of the service that is performed. This is also, to date, the least explored aspect of design firm management.

There is some mystery about why what industry calls quality assurance has been a neglected management area in design practice. One reason may be a traditional deference in the learned professions that makes review and constructive criticism of another's work seem demeaning. (Behind-the-back criticism, of course, is another matter.) Another reason may also be the classic concept, supported by both the education and registration process, of each engineer and architect as a "whole professional," fully capable of doing everything necessary to execute a project in the discipline. The most important reason may be a genuine lack of understanding about what it takes to sustain the creative process. This process, in the arts as well as the professions, has escaped synthesis, and perhaps designers have avoided exploring management of what they do because they themselves don't understand how they do it.

Nevertheless, the extension of architectual or engineering service from individual acts to a professional practice requires that the organization deliver a consistent quality of professional performance. This is the first responsibility of management.

Before quality of professional service can be managed, however, it must be defined, and there are a range of strong opinions, not at all in agreement, about what constitutes quality architecture or quality engineering. It may be defined as work that is either technically sound, functionally excellent, creatively distinctive, or some of all three. In practice, it is the different definitions of quality that distinguish one firm from another. No one can say that it is more or less important to concentrate on creative quality vs. technical quality. The market seems to have need for both types of performance, and a firm that concentrates on technical expertise may be just as successful as another firm that specializes in functional planning.

What is important is that the standard of professional performance be consistent from project to project on all the work the firm does. Firms where quality by this definition is high, do well regardless of size of organization or market specialization. When quality varies widely, the practice tends to lack stability and organization soundness. Such firms are often described as follows:

42

"They did a great job there years ago, but somehow they have never been able to do as well since. . . ."

"Whom you get to do your job in that firm determines what result you get. . . ."

The role of management in controlling quality of professional performance is to define a firm's standards and then find a way to manage all the work through the firm so that the process is repeated for all projects. This is easier said than done.

First, any effort by one professional to manage the performance of another treads on very sensitive ground. It must be done with attention to human factors as well as with great competence in the professional area involved.

Second, as mentioned earlier, not enough comparative experience is available to judge the success of different management mechanisms being tried by design firms.

The author's observations of design firms indicate that quality professional performance can best be managed by giving attention to one or all of the following areas:

1   Consistent standards for handling projects.
2   A consistent approach to leading (or following) the client.
3   Consistent patterns of quality review.
4   Clear responsibility for the last word.

There are a number of different ways that design firms are now approaching each of these areas. The more successful mechanisms are discussed below, area by area.

PROJECT HANDLING STANDARDS

There is a fine difference between standards that define how a project is to be carried out to achieve the highest professional performance and standards that define what must be done so rigidly that consistency is obtained, but individual initiative is stifled. The latter is typical of the bureaucratic approach: publish a manual of procedures and standards, and if everyone follows the manual exactly, every project will have roofs that are known not to leak, drawing standards that are known to be readable by contractors, and so on. This approach is widely used in government agencies and is popular with many engineers who believe there is only one optimum solution to every problem. Unfortunately, the approach also stifles independent judgment and often produces people who work "by the book" and are unable to give a professional answer to problems that don't happen to be in that book.

A better approach is to have project handling standards that define the process a design will follow, but do not specify the solution to be achieved. When such standards are carefully chosen for their ability to encourage exceptional professional involvement, the result can be enhanced professional performance. Some examples of such standards are given below.

Problem Statements

One of the most frequent causes of malperformance in design firms is development of solutions to a problem different from the real need of the client. To overcome this, some firms require that a written statement of the program and the objective of the assignment be prepared and approved by the client before design or technical work begins. If this statement is further subject to review and approval by all the professional leaders of the firm, before submittal to the client, great strides can be made in bringing the resources of the firm to focus together on the real problem.

Alternative Studies

In terms of the quality and depth of professional solutions generated by a firm, one of the most effective standards requires that at least two or three alternatives be seriously explored before a design scheme or technical approach is recommended on a project. This standard can apply equally well to creative architectural design schemes; alternative mechanical systems; or engineering cost benefit studies. The approach has wide-ranging implications in terms of encouraging professional open-mindedness, managing "prima donnaism," and in practical matters such as maintaining project budgets. If a firm is committed to being near the professional leading edge, no other single management procedure can be more effective in keeping it there than encouraging the exploration of alternatives. Furthermore, if the firm's policy is to share all alternatives, even discarded ones, with the client, additional benefits accrue both in terms of functional adequacy of the result and in leadership of the client (see below).

Graphic Standards

Every professional office should have standards for its graphic communication—ranging from letters, to job reports, presentation drawings, construction documents, specifications, and so on. These are the trademarks of a design firm, and their consistency is part of its flavor and image. While such graphic standards often tend to be prescriptive, other standards of graphic communication can be stimulative to professional performance. For example, one architectural firm that believes three-dimensional studies are important to site planning, requires that a site model be built of every project *before* design begins. If the standard also calls for the site model be large enough to include adjoining buildings on all four sides of the property, the standard may have some influence on the firm's performance in urban design. Similarly, many interior design firms require that color studies be made using actual samples of the materials under consideration. If it is further required that the swatches used be presented in actual proportion to their eventual scale in the space being designed, the result may be more sensitive design decisions.

There are probably several dozen additional standards of project handling that bear on quality professional performance in design firms. Their potential as a management tool has only been scratched at the surface. Any firm that gives major attention to the standards of its professional process can expect to receive benefits far in excess of the effort involved.

LEADING (OR FOLLOWING) THE CLIENT

Probably the one characteristic that most determines the type of work a professional design firm will do is its ability to lead or follow the client. This is not said in judgment of whether it is better to lead or follow.

There is need for professional firms that do what they are told by a client, and do it well. Clients who want colonial style office buildings or insist that all subdivision utilities be placed overhead are entitled to be served by design firms that will meet their demands without undue professional argument and will execute the work well.

There is also a need for design professionals who have the strength, the conviction, and the skill to lead clients to solutions that are often far beyond their original conception. This ability to lead the client is what produces four-lane bridges from initial projections that two lanes would be enough; 40-year life cycle specifications for public buildings originally budgeted for 15-year standards; and architectural design solutions that can reshape the lives of building users or replan a city core, even though the original request to the professional was merely to house a function.

The ability to lead is often seen as just a personal characteristic. There is no doubt that a professional with leadership skills can be very effective. Some are born with such skills; others can learn them through leadership training, even through such commercially pat vehicles as the Dale Carnegie Course. However, from a management standpoint, a firm can also develop organization standards for leadership that go beyond the skills of individuals.

Organization standards can make a simple letter typed on the firm's stationery carry substantial weight with public bodies, a client's board of directors, or even a court of law. A design firm that manages its leadership well will give the firm's professional "opinion" with care, and then will back up that opinion by fighting hard for what it believes is right. The firm may on occasion refuse or resign commissions when it feels its standards might be compromised, and it may also take substantial professional and financial risks in support of its opinion when it knows it is right.

Leadership should not be confused with professional arrogance. There are far too many self-proclaimed designers—especially among architects—who use arrogance as a substitute for leadership. Not only does this not work in the real world, but it can and does mislead younger professionals as they search for qualities that will help them to succeed in practice.

A design firm's management that sets standards for leading its clients will pay the most attention to how the firm takes positions and how it supports the positions it has taken. This may begin with a list of issues or subjects that may require "partnership" approval before the firm takes a stand, such as what commissions will be accepted; what construction budgets will be recommended to a client; suggestion of a totally new technical process to a client; or taking an appeal for variance of a building or safety code. It may also set standards for how the firm will communicate and deal with its clients. Will all client meetings be documented? Will the client be shown alternative schemes and studies to show how the professional reached the recommendation being made? (If the client is encouraged to play multiple choice, the firm is not leading the client.) Is the firm willing to share minutes of field problems that record the truth—even when they may reveal some oversight—or does the firm try to work these things out with the contractor and keep the client in the dark?

Again, a long list of standards of this sort can be developed by the management of the design firm. What they define is how the firm will lead its clients, and that definition will also say a lot about the quality of the firm's professional performance.

MANAGING QUALITY REVIEW

The classic way to ensure quality of performance is to organize the firm around a few key people—a good creative designer, a top production technician, and a wise field specialist who knows how to get work done and is respected by contractors. This is the basic operating structure of many firms. But quality in these firms is less managed than simply controlled by those who have the last word. The problem for such firms is that their capacity to sustain quality is limited by the capacity of the first principal who becomes overworked.

When such a firm attempts to grow beyond the capacity of the three specialists, it often creates project managers whose job it is to manage the client with one hand while steering the project through the firm's design, production, and construction departments with the other. Design firms have had success with the project manager approach, and the selection, development, and training of project managers has become the subject of manuals, seminars, and so on.

Meanwhile, clients have welcomed the project manager approach and have become increasingly sensitive to who will be the manager of their job when selecting engineers and architects.

It is important to recognize, however, that while the project manager approach deals primarily with the quality of *professional service* that is rendered this is not necessarily synonymous with quality of *professional performance*.

Quality of professional service, as defined by the project manager advocates, concentrates on getting the job done on schedule, on budget, and in compliance with all the program requirements.

Quality of professional performance, by definition, includes all the service considerations, but goes beyond them to encompass excellence of the technical, functional, and creative solutions delivered.

In this context, the management issue in design firms is not just who manages the project, but who—or what process—has the last word in determining that the standards of the firm are being met. One approach is to give the project manager the last word in both areas, which produces close control, quick decision-making, and clear accountability. This much free reign can also be a considerable motivator to the individual project manager, and is especially appealing to architects. The disadvantage is that firm's performance will vary with the project managers and clients tend to perceive these organizations as "Who-you-get-determines-what-you-get" firms.

Another approach is the strong department head organization where one individual has last-word responsibility for each function or discipline of project execution, such as design, production, specifications, structural, site, or interiors. This format creates strong consistency in each performance area and allows individual professionals to specialize and concentrate in the area of their greatest skills. This organization pattern appeals especially to engineers. However, whenever execution of a project involves more than one discipline or function—and the great majority do—coordination is difficult and one department's last word may contradict the word of another. Also, there is often conflict between department priorities and project priorities. In such organizations a project can get lost between departments, and project managers are often frustrated by their limited authority to push through discussions.

A third alternative to managing the professional process is often called the project review approach. Here the major professional aspects of a project are subject to a review by a group of key people before presentation to the client. In principle this is the optimum approach, because it encourages synergism and applies the collective skills of the firm to each project. It can also be fairly easy to manage, if there are clearly defined project milestones at which a project review is mandatory before work can proceed. A major limitation, however, is the nature of many design professionals to want to put their mark on everything they touch. If the review group fails to understand the difference between quality control and creative meddling, the projects can become diluted, and camels result. Group reviews are also cumbersome to arrange in a busy practice.

The project review approach to quality assurance works best when three ingredients are present:

1   The review group consists of compatible peers who enjoy working together, clearly understand the difference between "constructive review" and "critique," and are skilled in the human dynamics of working constructively with staff subordinates.

2   Reviews are always timed to occur at midpoint in the development of projects to avoid backing up and redoing the project.

3   Mechanically, the review group meets on a fixed day or at a fixed time every week and considers all projects that are ready for review at that time. This gives the project leaders a weekly scheduling target and leads to more efficient use of time. Although a project review organization makes use of many people, the process can be very cost efficient when it is conducted on this basis, because it sets weekly milestones that keep projects moving.

MANAGING THE LAST WORD

The complexities of modern design firm assignments, and the multidiscipline, teamwork requirements of design practice, have compounded the number and types of decisions required to execute every professional assignment. When partners, project managers, department heads, job captains, consultants, and other specialists are all involved, confusion about who is in charge may easily arise. Professional performance is then

Table 1   LAST WORD LIST (Broome Oringdulph, O'Toole, Rudolf & Associates)

This list is intended to clarify and expedite the office decision-making process. The list indicates the individual, or the group, who has the last word in final decisions.

Task	Last Word By[a]
Select principal-in-charge	The principals
Set fee	P.I.C.
Select team members	Q.C. for phase with office manager
Select consultants	P.I.C.
Set design production budget	P.M.
Approve contracts	P.I.C.
Approve construction budget	P.I.C.
Approve program	Q.C. design
Site analysis	P.M.
Set job schedule (calendar)	P.M.
Set master office schedule	Office manager and Q.C. for phase
Job staffing assignments	The principals with Office manager
Presentations to owner	Q.C. for Phase + P.M. and designer
Agency/code requirements	P.M. (sometimes J.C.)
Sign off on schematic design	Q.C. design
Sign off on design development	Q.C. design
Sign in on beginning of construction documents	Q.C. production and J.C.
Selection of building materials	Designer with review by Q.C. production
Sign off on construction documents	Q.C. production
Specifications	Q.C. construction
Bid list (if select)	Q.C. construction
Construction observation	Q.C. construction
Checking shop drawings	Project inspector
Design and product changes in construction	Q.C. construction

[a]P.I.C.—partner-in-charge; P.M.—project manager; Q.C.—quality control group; J.C.—job captain.

in jeopardy. Without exception, design firms that have confusing and overlapping decision structures not only have difficulty maintaining quality levels, but also become internally inefficient and often lose money in executing their projects.

One of the simplest and most effective devices for resolving such difficulties is to develop a "last word" list that defines significant milestones in typical projects and makes clear who has the last word or responsibility for a task. An example of a last-word list of an architectural firm is shown in Table 1.

The development of such a list can be an important management tool in itself. If all the project decision makers have a part in drawing up the list, initial collaboration and understanding will occur. One approach is to distribute to all persons in the firm a list of tasks with the decision assignments left blank and let them complete it as they believe the system should operate. Collecting these individual perspectives and resolving them into one standard for the firm can be a major undertaking that requires many meetings and the resolution of many conflicts. But the result can be extremely healthy in terms of internal communication, understanding, and down-the-road teamwork. Whenever these three aspects of a firm management are working well, professional performance cannot help but be improved.

This chapter has talked about the potential for management of professional performance. This is still an embryonic art. One day there may well be books written on the subject (plus, hopefully, some additional courses in design education curricula). Even without a textbook, however, the contemporary design firm manager can make great strides in this direction simply by recognizing that professional performance deserves management. In the end that means being committed, as a firm, to doing whatever you do as well as you possibly can. When someone is in charge of that simple goal, the quality of professional performance is beginning to be managed.

Chapter 6

MANAGING
THE MARKETING
PROGRAM

"Marketing is a top management function only to the extent that it supports and enhances the quality of architecture or engineering."

Martin C. P. McElroy
Marketing Director
TMP Associates

M anaging a marketing program is very different from doing the marketing. An earlier book by the author*—and a number of subsequent books by others—deal at length with how to do marketing of professional services at the tactical level, and there is no need to repeat that here.

Managing the marketing, however, is an art in itself. Only recently has enough experience with formalized marketing in design firms been accumulated to yield some knowledge about managing it. Marketing management involves the marketing plan; marketing staffing and organization; and monitoring marketing performance. This chapter tries to put these areas in perspective to enable the interested design professional to separate the managerial aspects of marketing from the tactical aspects.

What makes this particularly important is the growing discovery in firm after firm that knowing how to sell professional services doesn't at all guarantee a successful marketing program. The author's observation is that success in marketing of professional services is weighted by the following factors:

-5 to 10%—*Where You Sell It:* The choice of market, either by client/service type or geographically, is of major importance only in saturated markets. For the most part, there is room in every market for a better professional service.

-15 to 30%—*How You Sell It:* Clients are showing an uncanny ability to differentiate professionalism from hucksterism. How you sell is important when competition gets down to a short list of equally qualified firms, but clients are not buying many design services on salesmanship alone. If what you sell doesn't qualify you for that short list of firms, all the selling in the world won't often win the job.

-60 to 80%—*What You Sell:* The professional quality of what you do is clearly the most important factor in the success of a design firm's marketing program. Thus managing of marketing in a design firm involves a great deal more than supervising the job-by-job selling activity.

Marketing Architectural and Engineering Services, by Weld Coxe. Von Nostrand-Reinhold, 1971.

The relative emphasis of these aspects is further influenced by the market awareness of the firm's principals. Young founders who start a firm while very much in touch with the market may be outstripped if they become preoccupied with inside concerns as the practice grows. Thus, a firm's marketing program must also deal with how the policy makers receive outside stimulus on which to base market decisions.

THE MARKETING PLAN

If marketing is to be managed at all, a design firm must have a marketing plan that defines the following components:

Market(s):   What types of clients/projects will the firm pursue? In what geographic territory?

Capability: What services/strengths will the firm offer in these markets? (This is the single most important element of every professional marketing program.)

Message: How will the firm distinguish its capabilities from those of its competition, so the prospective client can know the difference? Can the firm articulate its strength and uniqueness?

Selling System: Will the firm rely on its reputation and references for work, or will it aggressively seek new opportunities? What will be the systems for lead finding; courting prospects; presentation of the firm's qualifications; interviews; and eventually closing the sale?

Merchandising: What sales tools, promotion, publicity, or advertising can be useful to the marketing program?

Marketing Organization and Budget: Based on the factors above, what roles are required, who will do them, and what will be the budget for time and out-of-pocket expense?

Marketing Goals: What results are desired? What yardsticks will be used to measure the progress of the marketing plan and to forecast the results?

Table 1 shows a simplified matrix that can be used to apply these components in developing a firm's marketing plan.

Future markets in which firm wants to be active		INDUSTRIAL	TARGETS OF OPPORTUNITY	MUNICIPAL	SCHOOLS		Markets
		1	80	5	21	Number of Present Clients (if any)	Markets
		50	—	3	—	Number of Potential Clients (on list to be contacted)	Markets
		5+	7.5	6	9	Capability in Relation to Competition (scale: 0–10)	Markets
		NEW DEPARTMENT LOW COST	WE ARE LOCAL	TRACK RECORD	TRACK RECORD	Message	Process
		PROSPECTING	COMMUNITY WORK	REPEAT/AND PROSPECTING	REFERRAL	Marketing Method (e.g., prospecting, referral, community work)	Process
		BC	JB	CA	AB	Assigned to:	Organization
		16 HOURS / WEEK	12 HOURS / WEEK	8 HOURS / WEEK	4 HOURS / WEEK	Assigned Effort (hours/$)	Organization
		40%	30%	20%	10%	Percent of Total Effort	Organization
		NEW BROCHURE	NEWSLETTER	USE PRESENT BROCHURE	USE PRESENT BROCHURE	Sales Tools (method and budget)	Organization
		30%	50%	10%	10%	Percent of Total Budget	Organization
		2 NEW CLIENTS OR $150,000	$200,000	$150,000	6 NEW CLIENTS OR $500,000	Goal (number of clients or $ volume)	Goal
		15%	20%	15%	50%	Percent of Present Workload	Long-Range Plan
		1	2	4	3	Priority	Long-Range Plan
		35%	20%	15%	30%	Percent of Future Workload	Long-Range Plan

Present markets in which firm is active

Note first that there is a separate plan-within-the-plan for each market. The strategy of the school market, for example, where the firm is top-heavy is to rely on repeat work from existing clients, and direct referrals, to find leads for new work. While this market will account for 50% of the firm's work for the coming year, it will consume only 30% of the marketing effort/budget because the emphasis of this plan is on diversification. In the industrial market, on the other hand, the plan calls for aggressive bird-dogging and prospecting to find leads and a heavy P.R. effort to build the firm's identity in that market. Thus the industrial market plan consumes 40% of the total budget, although it is only expected to yield 15% of the work for this period.

The long-range goals at the far right of the matrix are the key planning element. How much of the firm's work will come from each of its markets now and in the future? Design firm markets have distinct life cycles, and any firm striving for stability of workload will want to balance its mix of work so that it can ride out the ups and downs of individual markets. An exception would be a firm of specialists in one exclusive field, such as earthquake engineers. For such a firm, the alternative to diversification might be geographic dispersal, with branch locations chosen so that economic ups and down might balance.

The process by which the marketing plan is developed can be as important to success as the plan itself. Ideally, decisions about the selection of markets and the assignment/acceptance of primary responsibility for each market should be part of the collaborative goal-setting process described in Chapter 3.

MARKETING STAFFING AND ORGANIZATION

The success or failure of a defined marketing plan is in the hands of those who accept marketing roles in the firm. Their selection, motivation, and support is the job of management.

Some excellent professionals find selling to be unpalatable and cannot bring themselves to make a cold call on a faceless prospect. Others thrive on the chase, and would rather spend their time courting a new prospect than executing the job they won the day before. It would be folly to design a marketing plan that assigned bird-dogging roles to the first group and management roles to the second group.

In most design firms, the key players are a given group of professionals who have already chosen to work together. For such firms, marketing planning must begin with roles that are realistic and practical for the individuals involved.

The basic marketing functions that must be performed by one or several individuals are the following:

Closer: One who ultimately delivers the professional proposal to the client and wins the contract.

Courter: One who, during the get-acquainted stage, wins the confidence of the client in the firm's ability to do the job.

Lead Finder: One who knocks on doors or otherwise finds the leads to be courted and closed.

Coordinator: One who maintains the firm's selling resources and pulls together the statements of qualification, proposals, interviews, presentations, and so on, whenever they are needed in the selling process.

Marketing Manager/Director: One who is ultimately responsible for seeing that it all happens.

The division of these marketing functions in a design practice is based on the philosophy of the firm, market acceptance, and personal aptitude of the principals.

Closing

More often than not "Those who get the work, run the firm." It is almost a law of nature that professionals who bring in work either become principals of the firms in which they practice, or go into practice for themselves. Thus the role of the closer most frequently is held by a principal. Clients clearly prefer a closer who speaks with the firm's full authority. (There are some notable exceptions, especially in large engineering firms, where getting the job is the responsibility of hired closers who work in a marketing department, but these organizations tend to be selling the reputation and expertise created by a previous generation of principals. The ability of these "hired closer" marketing organizations to function consistently over time remains unproved.)

The management issue here is whether closers are also doers. A marketing organization composed of "closers who close" the projects and then hand them to "doers who do" them is quite different from an organization where the closer is also a doer who continues to manage the work after the sale. In the 1960s and early 1970s many marketing organizations built around charismatic closers and separate doer/project managers were very successful. In recent years, however, clients have demonstrated a clear preference for marketing organizations composed of closer-doers, where the professional making the sale can assure the client that he or she will be personally involved to a credible degree, during the execution of the project.

The significance of the closer/doer issue in marketing management lies in the ratio between the number of closer-doers in an organization and the maximum size at which the firm can efficiently operate. With marketing effort in architectural and engineering firms averaging 4−8% of total man-hours (see later in this chapter), it is clear that the closer in an organization with more than 15 people will have little time for doing except by delegating some of the marketing functions.

Surveys of marketing people indicate that the percentage of marketing time spent on the four functions is as follows:

15 to 20% for closing.
30 to 35% for courting.
25 to 35% for lead finding.
20 to 30% for coordination and resource preparation.
100% of marketing effort.

Thus it is clear that the degree to which a closer can delegate the nonclosing function is important to the efficiency of the entire organization.

Courting

The courting that occurs between lead finding and closing is often the most time consuming of all the marketing functions, but it can have the highest payoff in certain markets. A firm whose marketing program is "lead oriented" may successfully delegate the courting to the lead finder on a job-by-job basis. A firm whose marketing is "client oriented," that is, focused on long-term romancing of clients and agencies who regularly have work, will generally find courting to be the most effective if done by closer. This takes prime principal time, but the long-term payoffs from the relationships that can develop are generally worth it.

Lead Finding

In staffing terms, it is practical to delegate about 70% of all lead finding to a professional subordinate or hired marketing representative. It is important to understand the behavioral requirements of the birddog role, however, and to be realistic about expectations placed on persons performing this function. First, the ability to go out and knock on strange doors day after day to ferret out information requires a high tolerance for rejection. Furthermore, the birddog is required only to find the lead and then turn it over to a closer to make—or lose—the sale. Thus, birddogging is a "no win" role in which birddogs seldom can take singular satisfaction for the success of their efforts. One of the most distressing events in a birddog's life is the day he knows he should not go to the interview (where he might look like a "salesperson"), even though he has been almost solely responsible for the firm's getting the interview in the first place. If the closer then blows the interview by failing to follow the strategy that the birddog knew was correct, the disappointment can be devastating.

This combination of behavior traits (high tolerance for rejection and no need to "win") makes good birddogs very hard to find and harder to keep. Their care and feeding is a critical part of the marketing manager's function. Good birddogs need to be given a lot of operational latitude and they should never be required to handle such details as writing proposals or filing complex reports—tasks that are rarely compatible with the skills that make the role tolerable. A typical job/person description for a lead finder is included as Appendix 3.

Most design firms are finding that birddogging is not a realistic career position. Instead, it is often handled as a part-time function of either junior professionals on the way up or of closers or marketing coordinators as an adjunct to their primary roles.

Just how lead-finding and courting can—or cannot—be delegated depends chiefly on the individual markets being pursued. Public agency and institutional markets lend themselves to delegated or "hired" lead finders because they operate in an open environment where information about upcoming work is publicly accessible. Lead finding in private markets increases in difficulty based on the decision structure in the client organization. Large corporations and utilities are relatively more open than single entrepreneurs, such as developers. Thus the engineer specializing in subdivision development must generally do his own lead finding and courting, while the architect who specializes in correctional facilities can efficiently employ a birddog to find and qualify leads before getting the closer involved.

Coordinating

The marketing function that is the most easily delegated is resource coordination. The role of the marketing coordinator in design firms has grown so rapidly in recent years that it has become a para-profession of its own. The function can pay its way as a part-time activity in small firms with a half-dozen people, and it is becoming a common full-time activity in firms of 15 to 20 persons and more.

   The value of the marketing coordinator is that the functions assigned to the role tend to be the most efficient—and the most effective—when performed by one person. The marketing coordinator function can include involvement in marketing information, proposals and paperwork, presentation preparation, selling tools, public relations, research, and overall communication of the marketing effort among the principals of the firm. A typical job description for the marketing coordinator position is included as Appendix 4.*

Managing/Directing

One key person must have overall responsibility for managing the marketing program. This person can be a "manager" who facilitates the program; or he or she can become a "director", who tells everyone what to do. The character of the marketing program—and of the firm—will be decidedly different in each case.

   The reason for this has to do with the essence of the professional

*(An excellent manual entitled *The Marketing Coordinator,* by Janet Goodman, is sold by the Society for Marketing Professional Services, 1437 Powhatan, Alexandria, Virginia 22311).

relationship. If the client and the engineer or architect are to have a serious agency relationship, nine times out of ten that relationship will be cemented before or at the sale. In fact, closing the sale is usually the first act of agency between the two. Thus anything that comes between the client and the agent prior to the sale tends to color the total relationship thereafter, and often turns the professional service into a product or commodity.

The effects of this on marketing management are illustrated in Figures 1 and 2, which apply a marketing function to the matrix organization structure discussed in Chapter 4.

Figure 1 shows a directed marketing program. A strong marketing organization is assumed to have responsibility for finding clients and delivering them to design professionals, who appear at interviews by direction but are otherwise involved as little as possible before the sale.

In Figure 2, a managed marketing program, the leading design professionals in the firm are assumed to have primary responsibility for finding and signing up clients. The marketing organization exists to support and to coordinate, but the ultimate accountability for work under contract remains in professional hands.

A typical job/person description for a marketing director/manager is included as Appendix 2.

Over the past decade there has been a distinct evolution in the way design firms have staffed these marketing functions. In the 1960s, when formalized marketing was in its embryonic stage, the design firms that

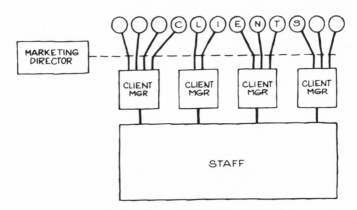

Figure 1   Directed Marketing Structure.

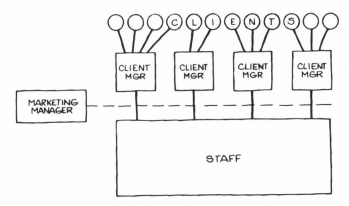

Figure 2 Managed Marketing Structure.

were the most successful at delegating a large share of the marketing effort employed specialized marketers as birddog/marketing directors. Over time, however, it became clear that this is not an enduring role. The best marketers found themselves in frequent conflict with design professionals over goals and strategy, and began pushing for a voice in the direction of the firms. Meanwhile, design professionals were learning that their role as closer is irreplaceable, and hence they were unwilling to give a marketer the power to tell them what to do. Faced with the likelihood that they would never be partners or principals, some of the better marketers have become management consultants, and most of the others have moved out of the design field after an average of 5 years. They are being replaced by an emerging breed of principal design professionals who acknowledge that the function of marketing management is essential to design practice and are trying to master it in addition to their professional roles.

At present, perhaps 20% of all architectual firms and 10% of all engineering firms have formalized marketing organizations with more than one person involved and with some differentiation in roles. The rest of the firms are either small practices, where the marketing is done entirely by the principal(s) without any formal plan, or they are larger organizations still living off a handful of loyal clients or a speciality that brings work to their door. Of the universe of firms that do have a structured marketing organization, the employment of specialized marketers is approximately as follows:

- About 10% of the firms have marketing managers/directors who are trained marketing professionals rather than design professionals wearing two hats. The role is a senior staff function, paying $30,000 to $50,000 in 1980 dollars, reporting directly to a managing principal or executive committee.
- About 20−25% of the firms, including about half of those that employ also a Marketing Director, have birddog/marketing representatives whose primary function is to seek and pursue leads for one or more closers. Many firms employ more than one marketing-representative, with each concentrating on a different market. This role pays $20,000 to $35,000 in 1980 dollars.
- About 95% of the firms have a designated part-time or full-time marketing coordinator. This role is frequently filled by a former executive secretary or by a person with P.R./writing skills. It was paying $15,000 to $30,000 in 1980.

This pattern seems likely to continue as marketing becomes a more and more regularized part of design practice. Principal design professionals will continue to be the closers, and in most firms one of them will accept the role of the marketing manager as well. Some larger firms will employ a marketing manager to free a principal from these functions. Every firm of over 10 or 15 persons will need a marketing coordinator to support the closers, draft proposals, and organize the marketing resources. A much smaller number of firms that specialize in fields where the role can be effective, will also employ marketing representatives to birddog those markets.

MARKETING BUDGETS

Average marketing costs in design firms, according to surveys, rose steadily for a decade until the late 1970s, when budgets leveled off. At that time the typical architectural firm with a formal marketing plan was spending 5−7% of gross fees on marketing, and the typical engineering firm was reporting marketing expenses in the range of 4−6% of gross fees. These averages are quite consistent in firms with annual gross fees of $300,000 (6−8 people) and up. The leveling off appears to be a consequence both of what clients are requiring in the way of marketing effort during the selection process and what design professionals are willing to exert to get work. It is reasonable to assume that the same levels will continue in the foreseeable future.

The most significant fact revealed by the surveys of marketing budgets is how the money is spent. With few exceptions, firms report that 70—80% of the marketing budget goes for personnel time and only 20—30% for direct expenses such as brochures, travel, and entertainment.

Extending these averages, we see that for every 20 people in a design firm, the equivalent of one full-time person must be devoted to marketing. In a 10-person firm, at least half of one person is required. It is the failure to accept this fact, more than anything else, that limits the success of many talented architectural and engineering firms. Design professionals who primarily enjoy doing the work may tend to neglect marketing so long as there is work to do. Since the lead time required to develop significant work is often 6 months to a year, however, such firms usually experience very erratic ups and downs in their workload.

Thus a major challenge of marketing management is to make sure that marketing is done consistently, especially during busy times.

MEASURING MARKETING PERFORMANCE

The least refined aspect of current marketing management in design firms is the measurement of performance toward the fulfillment of the marketing plan.

Product sales organizations have traditionally concentrated management effort on training salesmen, offering healthy commissions, and measuring performance in units sold.

The same carrot/stick methodology of sales management does not work for architectual and engineering service. There is no "product" that salesmen can be trained to sell again and again. Commissions have not been practical in design firms because of the team nature of the selling process. Rewarding a lead finder based on leads closed, for example, ignores the reality that the success of the sale is not in the lead finder's hands. Conversely, firms are reluctant to pay commissions merely for finding leads, some of which may never be closed. Compensation surveys consistently show that 95% or more of design firm marketers are employed on a straight salary basis, with regular profit sharing or bonuses. Most of the firms that reported paying commissions at one time have discontinued the practice after a few years.

Measuring results after contracts are signed is far too late in the marketing sequence to assure management that the process is going well. It is becoming apparent that it is preferable to manage the steps in the marketing sequence and to let the end result—the contracts—take care of itself. Among the most practical units of measurement are the following:

List Preparation: Every closer and lead finder in the firm should have a list of prospects to be contacted. This may be a small list of new prospects that a lead finder has prepared to open a new market or it may list known past clients with whom the firm wants to maintain contact. The marketing manager should know that each person with a marketing role has prepared a list, and should review and approve the lists.

Contact Frequency: Another measure of performance is the rate at which persons on the list are contacted. It is not of concern that one closer makes one contact a week, another closer makes only one a month, and the lead finder makes three a day. Each marketer should be allowed to set his or her own pace and quota. But each should have a quota, so that the manager has a yardstick by which to monitor performance.

Leads Found: The number of leads found from a certain number of contacts is not a valid measure of the person making the contacts. It does indicate the quality of the list, however, and the manager may suggest revising lists if the yield is low. Overall, the manager should keep count of the total number of live leads known to the firm. Such a count, as it grows and shrinks, is an excellent barometer of the total prospecting effort—and the outlook for eventual sales.

Size of Leads: A lead finder may produce a high volume of live prospects, but they might include too many small feasibility studies and other cats and dogs that do not justify the marketing effort. In such cases, it is often practical to set a lead finder's goal in terms of size (e.g., projects that exceed a certain minimum fee) and to manage the list preparation and contacting effort on that basis.

Short Lists from Leads: A measure of the quality of courting, and another measure of the quality of leads, is the ratio of the number of times the firm is short listed to the number of leads seriously pursued. This ratio is particularly helpful in controlling the marketing budget, because the cost of pursuing a lead, including the time needed to court the decision makers and expenditures for a detailed brochure of qualifications, can easily reach thousands of dollars each time. On finding that the firm is not making a realistic share of short lists, the manager may set up more selective standards for choosing the leads that are to be seriously pursued.

Batting Average: Mathematically, a firm is breaking even on its marketing effort if it wins jobs in direct proportion to the number of competitors on the short lists. For example, if there are five firms on the typical short list, a 20% success rate means breaking even. Keeping score on the firm's yield from competitive situations is a good measure of its competitiveness; its tactical selling strategies; its basic professional capabilities, or all these.

The importance of having such marketing yardsticks cannot be overemphasized. In the typical design practice, the marketing plan is always aimed toward mid- and long-range targets. If the manager waits to measure success until these targets have been hit, it is far too late to avoid the penalties of shortfall. Marketing performance should be measurable—and measured—at least quarterly in small firms and more frequently in larger organizations. When this happens, marketing is being managed.

Chapter 7

MANAGING
HUMAN RESOURCES

"He's the prototypical, hard-to-manage creative person."

W. Ennis Parker, Jr., AIA
President
Heery & Heery

An organization is only as good as its people. Since design organizations are by nature people intensive, one would think that human resources would have been the first area of design firm operations to receive serious management attention. Not so. The management revolution in design practice began with architects focusing on marketing in the late 1960s and engineers focusing on financial/business management. In the 1970s the reverse occurred: engineers became concerned with marketing and architects turned their attention to finance and business. Until the late 1970s human resources remained largely taken for granted, rather than managed.

It is clear, however, that human resources will become a major focus of management concern in design firms in the early 1980s. The reasons are threefold.

First, there is a serious shortage of trained talent. During the recession of the mid-1970s, consulting practice could not make use of all graduating architects and engineers, and a major crop of potential talent (who found work in government and industry or pursued alternate careers) was lost to design firms. When the market came back to life late in the decade, design firms could not find all the experienced talent they needed and for the first time began to consider programs to retain the talent they already had. In the meantime, qualified people had begun showing a clear preference for working in firms with better management and career development programs.

Second, for decades it has been assumed that a licensed engineer or architect with certain experience (e.g., 5 years on the boards, or 3 years as a job captain; or whatever) is universally qualified to do that level of a job wherever employed. Thus an expanding firm in need of, say, a project manager, two job captains, and four draftpersons would hire people with equivalent experience, put them to work on the jobs at hand, and expect fully adequate performance. More recently, however, it has become clear that such hirees will at best deliver the standard of performance learned from their previous employer—and not necessarily what the hiring firm has sold its client. Consequently, design organizations have begun to recognize that they must properly select, train, and develop their own human resources if they expect to achieve their particular standard of service.

Finally, the increasing body of government laws requiring compliance on personnel policies have forced employers to give more serious attention to human resources.

The trend in design firms toward more serious management of their human resources is very timely—for it is coming just as the behavioral sciences have reached the point where managers now have real tools to help people to maximize their potential. The subject of managing human behavior—at both personal and functional levels—has been gaining attention in Western society as we have been successful in meeting most material needs (for food, clothing, shelter, etc.) When those needs were still paramount, organization managers were able to rely on the material carrot to motivate workers to perform. We now have for the first time a society where the fulfillment of most material needs is taken for granted and, instead, motivation is sought from such nonmaterial values as purpose, responsibility, recognition, and satisfaction. Since these values are particularly important to design professionals, what the behavioral scientists are learning about managing has direct and timely application in design firms.

Even though the subject is timely, don't look for easy answers. Human resource management is still an emerging discipline. New books are being written daily about various aspects of the field. No design firm manager can be fully conversant with the state of the art. But this is an area where even a little application of an advanced technique can produce major improvements in an organization. The manager who is aware of the new ways to motivate, develop, and communicate with people and looks for techniques that can be applied in the organization, will benefit greatly from the effort.

It is important to recognize that most organizations—in all fields of endeavor—operate at somewhat less than the full potential of their people. In an optimum system, everyone is moving in the same, clear direction and all energy goes into furthering the mission at hand. There are few optimum systems. In more typical organizations, considerable energy is consumed as people rub against one another trying to find ways to work together, and the resulting output is some percentage less than the aggregate potential of the input. In the worst cases, immobilization occurs. (Selection officers in the U.S. Postal Service tell of an interview they conducted in the offices of an established small architectual firm. The question came up: Who would run this project if you were commissioned to do it? One principal replied: "I will!" The other principal immediately exploded: "Like hell you will. . . . You take all the good jobs away from me. . . . I intend to run this job. . . ." The resulting argument between the principals continued to grow more intense as the federal officials slipped away and began looking elsewhere for a firm to do the job.)

The object of management is to help keep the firm's human resources functioning as close to optimum as possible.

To do this with any degree of effectiveness, it is essential to recognize that *managing* behavior is in no way synonymous with *controlling* it. To achieve the ends of the organization, the manager need only know how to help others manage their existing behavior—not manipulate it.

A design organization that is concerned with maximizing its effectiveness should have a human resource plan. Like other management plans, it should identify what is needed in the human resources area to help achieve the short- and long-range goals of the firm, and it should define the specific strategies selected to work toward those ends.

ASSESSING THE ORGANIZATION CLIMATE

To develop a human resource plan, it is often wise to start by assessing the existing human resources climate in the organization to see how the firm compares to the optimum system.

For example, each member of the organization—from secretary, to draftsperson, to managing principal—might be asked to write answers to the following questions:

- What can the organization do *more of* in order for you to be the most effective in your role?
- What can the organization do *less of* in order for you to be the most effective?
- What do you want to continue to be the *same* as at present in order for you to be the most effective in your role?

Such a survey, honestly answered, can yield a list of "Mores," "Lesses," and "Sames" that will serve as an excellent starting point for developing a human resources plan.

A more sophisticated device for measuring the human resources climate in an organization is a survey developed by Dr. Rensis Likert, one of the original applied behavioral scientists, at the University of Michigan. It attempts to average the views of all personnel into an index of

LIKERT ORGANIZATIONAL SURVEY

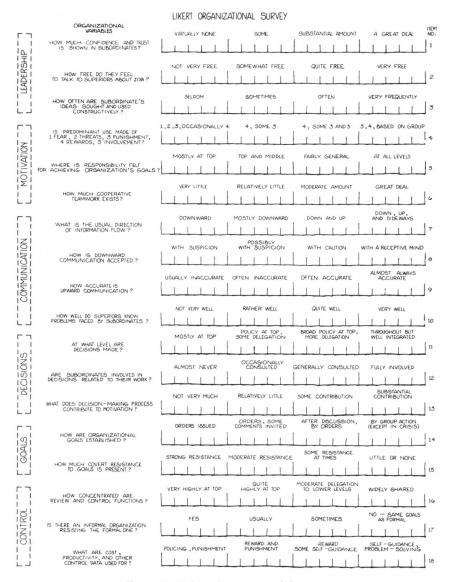

Figure 1 Likert Organizational Survey.

actual organization climate. The Likert survey has the added benefit that it can be used like a thermometer: it can be retaken annually to measure the progress being made toward the goals of the human resources plan. Tests by Likert in thousands of organizations have demonstrated its relative accuracy and its usefulness as a management tool.

Figure 1 shows the Likert survey questionnaire. It measures 18 variables grouped in 6 areas: leadership; motivation; communication; decisions; goals; and control. Accompanying each of the variables is a continuum of answers reading from left to right.

In using the survey, each staff member is asked, anonymously, to rate each variable by placing the letter N on the continuum where the organization is perceived to be *now* and the letter O to indicate where the organization *ought* to be.

Figure 2 is a composite of the Likert surveys compiled in a typical design firm. The jagged line down the left side represents the composite of the *Now* entries, and the jagged line to the right is the composite of the *Ought* entries. Each variable now tells something specific about the climate in the organization.

Thus the answers in item 3—"How often are subordinate's ideas sought and used constructively?"—indicate that this firm's staff members think they are *now* "often" consulted and that this is very close to what they feel it *ought* to be.

Conversely, item 14 reveals the staff feeling that goals are *now* largely set by "orders" and that they *ought* to be much more involved. The spread here of more than 10 notches on the continuum flags an area where planned action could yield real benefits to the organization.

An additional output of the Likert survey is its mirroring of the type of management style at work in the organization. Likert does this by characterizing each of the systems in the continuum:

System 1	System 2	System 3	System 4
Autocratic	Benevolent/ bureaucratic	Consultative	Participative/ democratic

Likert's studies reveal that any gradual movement of the composite *now* items to the right on the continuum—in any organization—yields long-term benefits in every measure of organization performance: produc-

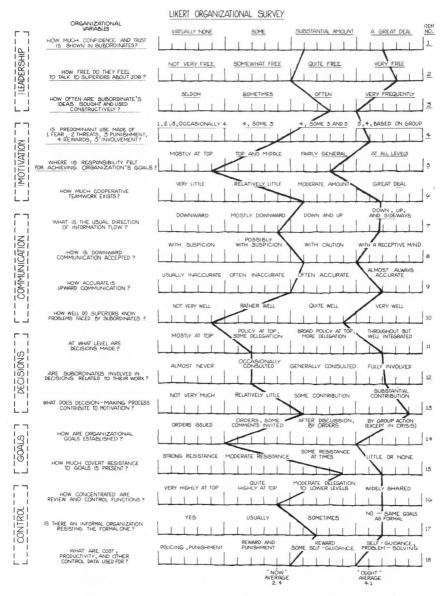

Figure 2   A Composite of Likert Organizational Surveys.

tivity, quality, profitability, morale, reduced turnover, and so on. Thus the manager can use the Likert survey as a direct tool to identify areas for action, which will yield broad benefits to the organization.

In the firm used as the example in Figure 2, the average of the *now* items in all 18 variables is given at the bottom—a reading of 2.4 on Likert's scale. The *ought* entries have an average of 4.1. A manager developing a plan to move that organization in the *ought* direction would begin by focusing on the variables that are shown to be holding down the average—items 14, 10, and 5. If management can accept the reality of the answers, it can be relatively easy to develop plans for each of these areas. For example, the firm may decide to hold a staff retreat to seek input on firm goals (item 14); listen more openly to staff problems at that retreat, and at other times (item 10); and begin delegating more responsibility in important areas of the firm's management (item 5). If these actions were the focus of a human resources plan for the coming year, a retake of the Likert survey 12 months down the road should give a picture of what results have been achieved.

It is best to use the Likert survey only if the firm's manager of human resources has had some guided exposure to it or has read Likerts' books. *

Likert emphasizes that even though organizations can be successful anywhere on the continuum, research has demonstrated that they will be more successful if they move incrementally to the right. It is therefore clear that the more open a management system is, and the more the members of the organization feel involved in that system, the better the system will perform for its members. Likerts' book pursues the broader implications of this in some detail, and is especially worth reading by those whose management style may be part of the problem (see also Chapter 12).

THE HUMAN RESOURCES PLAN

All the foregoing addresses the longer-range aspects of a human resource plan. At the day-to-day level, a plan should also incorporate basic personnel policies, including standards for acquiring staff and for ongoing management of individuals in the organization on a one-to-one basis.

---

*New Ways of Managing, by Dr. Rensis Likert, McGraw-Hill, 1974.

Such ongoing management attention is especially beneficial in these areas:

Role Definitions: Having a clear understanding of what is expected of each member of the staff, and what staff members expect of management.

Performance Review and Development: Having procedures that make a "personnel review" process a genuinely productive tool for both manager and subordinate, rather than a chore to be postponed whenever possible.

Compensation: Using rewards in proper context within the overall system for managing personnel.

Training and Development: Having formalized programs to help develop the firms staff to ever-advancing levels of professional competence and performance.

The level of sophistication at which each of these areas is now being managed in design firms varies tremendously. Role definitions and compensation are probably the most advanced, although far short of their potential; performance review is currently receiving the most serious attention; and only a handful of firms have reasonably sophisticated training and development programs. Progress made in any one of the areas can be helpful. The discussion of each area below cannot begin to cover the range of possibilities for better management of human resources, but is intended to illustrate the potential that can be derived if attention is paid to the different areas.

ROLE DEFINITIONS

It is sometimes interesting—and it would be entertaining were it not so serious—to compare management's description of a group of jobs with the descriptions of those holding the positions. A management consultant was once asked to interview a sampling of employees in a large firm, which included a dozen people that management classified as "draftsmen." When the consultant completed the interviews, however, he found he had talked to, by their definition, 8 "assistant job captains" and 4 "assistant designers." When the firm later published an internal telephone directory by job classification, which listed 22 "draftsmen" and 9 "junior draftsmen," all hell broke lose; the office of the managing principal was filled with dissatisfied employees, and 3 left the company.

It should be apparent that titles have very little to do with defining performance. If people like the status of an important-sounding title, the title can be a very inexpensive satisfier. This is why a bank with 500 or 600 people may have 150 "vice-presidents."

It is much more important that manager and employee have a clear description of the functions each expects of the other. This may sound like a cliché, but consider the following conversation common in distressed organizations:

Manager: *"Why aren't you doing what I want you to do?"*
Subordinate: *"You've never told me what that is!"*
Manager: *"Well, you should know!"*

All that is needed to avoid this scenario is clear and frequent communication about the function to be performed and the part that each party is expected to play in carrying it out. Such a role description can seldom be documented once and cast in stone. The old textbook approach to management suggested that organizations could be created out of a manual of written job descriptions by simply finding people to fit each page. Now it is generally recognized that neither people nor functions are static— especially not in a design firm. Thus role descriptions are likely to be constantly evolving. The sensitive manager will regularly review and revise with subordinates both their job description and that of the manager.

The most effective way to accomplish this is not to tell the subordinate that "This is what I want you to do," but: "This is the result I want achieved. What will you do to help achieve it—and what do you want of me to help you do that?"

In well managed organizations, supervisors from the top down are trained over time to define roles in this manner. Such role descriptions are best written down so that they can be referred to later at review time (see below), but they can also be verbal so long as there is no disagreement later. This yields a system where expectations and subsequent performance are as close together as possible.

PERFORMANCE REVIEW AND DEVELOPMENT

For many managers perhaps the most unpleasant chore is "personnel reviews"—the periodic assessment of the performance of one's subordinates, usually resulting in adjustments in compensation. Design professionals have special difficulty with the review process because, not having started their careers in large business organizations, they seldom have previous experience in it. Moreover, design professionals are generally more task than management oriented and are impatient at having to take time from the job at hand to deal with their subordinates on a long-range developmental basis.

On the other side of the transaction are design firm employees who view with anxiety the process of communicating with management about job performance and who are happy to settle for the least painful way of receiving their annual raise. Those who have clear career ambitions will usually pursue their own goals by changing jobs as necessary to move up the ladder—rather than by challenging the employer to meet their needs.

In many design firms, therefore, turnover is higher than it need be and growth—in capability terms—of the firm itself is limited by the lack of opportunities for the people to grow. In design practice today the "personnel review" process is widely neglected, often mishandled, and only rarely implemented at or near its potential as a vital management tool for developing the firm.

Experience has demonstrated, however, that the firms that have effective systems for performance review and development have made great strides in individual proficiency, internal communication, teamwork, morale and, consequently, overall performance of the professional organization.

To have such a system, management must agree on three principles:

1   The goal of such a process is developmental—not judgment of the past. All people grow, and a process that encourages them to develop their potential is much easier to accept than one that is based on reviewing a report card of past performance.
2   It is essential that both managers and subordinates agree that the only significant measure of any working relationship is output. Such factors as personality, attitude, appearance, and life style have no place in the performance review process unless

they directly affect output. (Of course, in the close personal environment of many design firms some of these factors may get in the way of productive working relationships. Few of us can really work effectively with someone we do not like. The point is that no review or development system can deal with such factors. They must be handled during initial hiring, by transfer to other roles, or by amicable parting on the basis of personality, not performance).

3   Compensation is a by-product of a development process, not the purpose of it.

There are a wide variety of seminars, procedures, handbooks, and so on, designed to instruct managers in systems for personnel performance review and development. Almost any system will yield some worthwhile benefits. Most design firms will want to assign a manager to investigate alternative systems before adopting one that best fits the needs of their organization. One key element in the choice of a system is the amount of time required to implement it. Some of the most sophisticated systems require that a manager spend 8 to 16 hours annually with each subordinate in activities solely concerned with performance review and development (this might consist of a 2- to 3-hour initial planning session, followed by quarterly update meetings of 1 or 2 hours each, plus a few minutes each day in "our board" touching base). Few design professionals are willing to deduct this much time from project tasks to dwell on the development of the people they work with. Moreover, many self-motivated professionals do not need such attention to keep them productively on the team. But there is a definite ratio between the time devoted to performance review and development and the results achieved. If only a limited amount of time is going to be committed to developing each employee each year, this should be kept in mind when choosing or designing a system for the firm.

Several elements are common to all effective developmental systems, which, once they are incorporated in the agenda of performance review meetings with staff, can lead to dramatic results:

1   Define the key results expected from the role, not how to achieve them (see role description above). Write down these key results in words that both parties understand.

2   List measurable work objectives planned to achieve the key

results. It is best that the subordinate generate the first draft of these events. But the events must be stated in terms that are measurable by future performance. (If the key result for a draftsperson is working drawings, the measurable work objectives might deal with a specific number of drawings to be completed over time, or with a specified minimum number of revisions required as a consequence of poor coordination. If the key result is design, the measurable work objectives might deal with the number of submissions necessary to gain client approval, or with meeting the design budgets, or even with the number of projects deemed worthy of submission for design awards.) The essential point is that work objectives must be measurable over a defined period of time, and must include the objectives of both parties for improvement.

3 Reach clear agreement on what future compensation and rewards will be if performance (after the next review) is fully adequate as defined. It must also be clear that less than fully adequate performance may lead to postponement of that compensation and that better than fully adequate performance will be the basis for future advancement.

When such a system is working well, it gives the subordinate and the manager a clear understanding of the performance that is expected *in advance*, thus removing anxiety and unexpected criteria from the next review. This in turn allows the subsequent reviews to become primarily developmental, as manager and subordinate work to define new measurable work events that will continue to improve performance.

At these review sessions, subordinates and managers should strive to be clear and honest about their career objectives for each other. It should be no sin for an employee to admit, in advance, intentions to stay with a firm only a few years. Conversely, the manager should feel free to define the limitations this may impose on advancement as compared to an employee intending to make a career in the firm. It is also entirely proper for a subordinate to say: "I want to be a principal by the time I am 40." It is equally in order for the manager to say: "We don't expect to have a vacancy for your talents here, but you are welcome to continue as a project manager as long as you like, and in that role you can expect to advance to x type of work and y compensation."

What makes such a process particularly developmental is that both parties agree in advance how performance is to be measured. Whenever a subordinate requires additional training or staff support to reach an objective, it can be planned in advance. And most of all, it is the subordinate who defines the work events, so that the opportunity for innovation and suggestion of new techniques is always open from the bottom of the organization upward. No wise manager could ask for more.

COMPENSATION

As mentioned above, compensation should be a by-product of the performance review and development process, not the purpose of it. There is a real place for incentive compensation in a human resources plan, but in design firms it is most effective when seen as an organization incentive rather than as an individual incentive.

To understand this concept it is first necessary to see basic compensation as completely separate from incentive compensation. There is a basic market value for virtually every skill in every marketplace and within every firm. The manager must offer competitive compensation, or the employees will go where they can get it. This is basic compensation. It is subject to limited adjustments for experience, tenure, and fringe benefits, but is essentially fixed by the laws of supply and demand, and firms can budget their costs accordingly. Attempts to play games with base compensation, by substituting a bonus or "extra" fringe benefits such as car allowances or large pension plans, are generally counterproductive and often end up costing more. The same is true of attempts to manipulate such normal and customary benefits as vacations or health insurance. Firms that develop unusual formats for reducing basic compensation usually do so in an attempt to defer some of that base into profit sharing or a tax shelter (e.g., pension). But once started, such benefits must be offered to new recruits as well, and it is generally difficult to persuade a newcomer to take several thousand dollars less in basic compensation in exchange for some promised fringe rewards down the road. The soundest practice is to have basic compensation plans that are competitive in your market, and be able to say to all present or prospective employes something like the following:

> "We try to keep our salaries competitive with what you may be offered elsewhere. The current range for your position in this firm is

x to y . As you gain experience and skill we would expect to move you up toward the top of thát limit. If you advance to _____ position, the range for that role increases to z . In addition to this base compensation, our normal benefits include _____ ."

Under such a base compensation policy, it also becomes easier during performance reviews to tell staff members what increment (other than cost of living) will be available in recognition of fully adequate performance.

There is much merit also in setting base compensation for principals and partners at their fair market value for the function performed. This is a good way to create a policy of unequal principal salaries, which, where applied, can resolve a number of other structural and management issues.

Incentive compensation is an entirely different matter. It has wide application in design firms because of the nature of professional practice as a fee-paid service. There is considerable question, however, whether incentive compensation can be best applied to motivate individual performance or, rather, to induce and reward collective performance.

In business there are often roles where individual performance can be independent of an organization—such as product sales, or piecework—and incentive or contingent compensation can then be quite effective. In professional practice, however, there are few independent roles that are not held by principals. Marketing representatives cannot sell independently of those who will deliver the service; project managers cannot execute assignments without the collaboration of other specialists or department heads. Design firms have struggled for years to find formulas for allotting incentive compensation, with most plans being abandoned because of the difficulty of assessing the individual—as opposed to the team—contribution.

Instead, most design firms use a bonus system, with the amounts being set at the discretion of one or more principals. This can be effective, provided that the principal making the discretionary judgments is unusually fair and astute (and provided that staff members do not compare notes on what they received in the year-end envelope).

Incentive compensation can also be viewed as a collective reward to the team that earns the profits. It is then prorated on the weighted contribution of each function that makes up that team. This is a relatively new approach to incentive profit sharing, but design firms that have experimented with it are enthusiastic about its potential to deal with the shortcomings of other bonus plans.

In practice, such a system works as follows. First, the key roles that have the most to do with performance leading to profitability are identified. In a truly egalitarian firm everyone may be included, but generally it is those classified as "associates," "principals," or some similar designation for key personnel.

These functions are then weighted by the estimated value of each to the total profitability of the firm. That weight is expressed in terms of a percentage of base compensation. For example, the functional weights might look like this:

Class of Personnel in Profit-Sharing Pool	Incentive Compensation as a Percentage of Base Compensation
"Closer" principals	80%
Management principals	60%
Project managers	50%
Marketing representatives	45%
Job captains	20%
Etc.	

With the base compensation of all the individuals performing these functions established as previously outlined, there is no need to adjust incentive compensation for individual performance. The adjustments have been covered in the base compensation, and the incentive formula will reward the full team proportionately. Those whose performance has not reached the level where they qualify for a share of profits are simply not yet included in the pool.

Once the weighted factors have been applied, a total goal for incentive compensation can be calculated, individual by individual, as shown in Table 1. In this example, a total incentive goal of $287,000 is obtained. More importantly, each person's individual percentage of that pool is also known. Thus earnings that are larger or smaller than the goal can be divided accordingly.

Establishing the size of the pool to be divided requires consideration of what is due the owners of the firm as a return for their risk and investment. Innumerable variables, mostly tied to personal history go into this decision, but in absolute terms one formula might be as follows:

> *The incentive compensation pool will equal the actual amount of the goal, if earned, or 50% of profits, whichever is greater.*

Table 1   Profit-Sharing Pool Formulation

Participants by Class[a] and Base Compensation	Class Incentive Factor	Extension (% × Base)	Share In Pool
Closer principals	80%		
A. $75,000		$60,000	20.9%
B. $75,000		60,000	20.9%
C. $55,000		44,000	15.3%
Management principal	60%		
D. $60,000		36,000	12.5%
Project managers	50%		
E. $40,000		20,000	7.0%
F. $35,000		17,500	6.1%
G. $30,000		15,000	5.2%
Marketing representatives	40%		
H. $40,000		16,000	5.6%
I. $25,000		10,000	3.5%
Job captains	20%		
J. $22,500		4,500	1.6%
K. $20,000		4,000	1.4%
Profit-sharing goal		$287,000	100%

[a]The pool is assumed to be limited to selected individuals chosen by their contribution; does not apply to all staff holding the titles in each class.

In this approach, the first people to be rewarded if there are any profits are those who earned it. Owners receive profits only when they exceed the minimum goal. The reverse can also be argued—that owners should get some compensation off the top. Such a formula might read:

The incentive compensation pool will equal 50% of profits, if earned, up to the actual amount of the pool.

The choice depends on the structure and personalities of the individuals setting the organization goals. Whether or not the firm is heavily involved in work subject to federally audited overhead is also a factor, since bonus plans must be carefully structured to qualify as an overhead expense. What is important about the suggested approach to profit sharing is that it establishes a workable formula for incentive compensation that key personnel can rely on in advance and that it is designed to foster collaboration and teamwork. Incentive compensation that accomplishes this is a working tool of the human resources plan.

TRAINING AND DEVELOPMENT

At this writing, the author knows of no training and development plan in operation in any design firm in the United States that could be a model for others to follow. Compared to business and industry, where growing one's own personnel by internal training has become a refined management activity, design firms are only beginning to experiment with the potential of seriously developing some of their own staff.

The major benefits of having a formal training and development program have already been described: It is the best way to ensure that the organization will deliver to clients what the firm is selling as its own unique capabilities. There are other benefits as well: it helps to attract the best young talent to the firm and greatly improves internal communication and teamwork.

It remains to be seen what design firms will learn in the years ahead about the relative cost/benefits of effort applied to personnel training and development. Probably only the largest firms will invest in staff training specialists. The average firm's training program is likely to consist of a composite of procedures, including some of the following (all of which are working well in firm's that have tried them):

1   **Formal, regular recruiting of young talent.** Identifying the schools that produce the caliber of people you want enables you to establish a policy of hiring one or more employees from each graduating class of that school. Cultivate the dean so that your firm becomes known and the faculty can help to spot the most likely candidates for you. Use a recent graduate from your staff as your primary recruiter. Offer the recruits a certain defined learning experience (by way of rotation of assignments) during their first years with you. Don't expect to keep all you hire. (Those that leave will be your best advocates wherever they

go.) The object is to bring in a regular flow of new blood to keep the organization dynamic and up to date. When that occurs there should be no difficulty in keeping the very best as future leaders.

2 **Orienting all newcomers.** One design firm has all new employees, on their first day with the firm, view a comprehensive slide show similar to that shown to prospective clients. You can't invest too much time in letting a new employee know what the firm is selling and how it works. One way to reduce the orientation burden on key principals is by a buddy system that pairs each newcomer with an older staff member who becomes responsible for the orientation. Don't use the same "old hands" all the time. There can be real value in having everyone in the firm do orientation, in rotation. An induction process that begins with thought-out orientation of original employees will repeat itself over the years without its becoming an undue burden.

3 **Rotating job assignments of new staff.** Most firms make some effort to rotate technical staff—a draftsperson may get a 6-month assignment in the field, for example—but frequently nothing further is done. Once assigned, the individual is left to his or her own devices to learn—or not to learn—what the new role is all about. To avoid this, a senior staff member in each field should be assigned as the "mentor" for that function and management should specify to both newcomer and mentor the results it expects from each rotation. Furthermore, the process can be expanded beyond technical roles. One medium-size engineer-architect identified six young staff members, all under age 32, as future potential top management. The six were asked to help design their own training program. They are (in turn) "shadowing" each of the firm's present managers for 6-month terms; they sit in on many executive meetings; and they hold periodic evening bull sessions at the home of the firm's founder—all while carrying on their regular full-time assignments.

4 **Quality control committees.** One design firm has developed a series of committees responsible for keeping on top of advances in the state of the art in defined areas, such as specifica-

tions, production techniques, design, and financial management. The committees—everyone on the 30-person firm serves on one of them—have a budget for research travel and seminars and must prepare an annual report to the firm on what has been learned as well as a plan for the techniques that will be implemented in the firm in the coming year.

5   **Brown-bag show-and-tell luncheons.**   In far too many firms of all sizes some staff members don't know what the firm is really doing. They may know, for example, that the firm is working on a treatment plant for a client, but not about the nature of the assignment, how it was won, its key problems, or how solutions to the problems are being developed. One easy way to share such information is to have a regular (weekly is best) in-house luncheon where everyone can hear one project team explain a current assignment. Don't wait until the job is over and all the problems solved. It can be more interesting to staff—and produce good input—if the first show-and-tell is at a specified early point in the job, such as the end of programming. This type of training program can be accompanied by a policy of taking the staff on formal inspections of completed projects whenever practical.

6   **Budgets for continuing education.**   Every firm should budget for such activities as attending seminars, and should see that the right people find time to participate. For this investment to pay off, the attendee, upon returning, should report what was learned to a larger group and should recommend specific actions the firm can take to implement the new knowledge.

These few examples are intended to illustrate how much can be done with little effort when training and development are made a part of the human resources plan. Much, much more is possible if a firm commits itself to developing its own staff.

This chapter will have accomplished its purpose if it has demonstrated the value of human resources planning in design firm management. The effort needed to do this well, however, far exceeds the time that many design firm principals care to devote to management. This is a human resources problem in itself. The task-oriented design firm principal who is most happy when filled to the brim with clients and project respon-sibilities has just as much right to be motivated as each member of the staff. It thus becomes a choice between doing what one enjoys most or managing the organization. The ideal—a design professional who also enjoys management—is rare. The answer lies in recognizing the dilemma (see also Chapter 12), making a choice, and then either holding the organization to the size defined by that choice or delegating much of the human resources management to others who like it. Design practice is a people business, and all people work best when they are motivated and enjoying what they are doing. Isn't that the bottom line of it all?

Chapter 8

MANAGING
THE NUMBERS

*One architect to another: "What would
you do if you had a million dollars?"*

*Reply: "I'd continue practicing
architecture until it was all gone."*

Cartoon

The use of financial information as a management tool in design firms is still very much misunderstood. Some professions find the discipline of understanding the numbers aspects either threatening or irrelevant, and simply ignore the potential of financial management systems. Others, are aware of the value of financial systems, but may frequently be inadequately advised about what reports to receive and which controls to watch; consequently they may become frustrated and confused by the whole subject.

Part of the reason is historical. Serious efforts to develop financial management systems especially for design firms did not begin until the mid-1960s. By the late 1970s probably no more than 15–20% of the engineering firms and 5–10% of the architectural firms in the United States were using financial information as an important management tool. Countless other firms were by then keeping manual or computerized financial records, but were making very little use of them except to bill clients and prepare tax returns.

The basic cause lies in the bottom line differences discussed in Chapter 1. Most financial systems have been developed by businesses to serve business considerations—leading to a quantitative bottom line. Design professionals who are motivated by a qualitative bottom line often find the aims of such a system in conflict with their values, hence overlook the system's potential as a useful tool. Even well-managed businesses today recognize that financial information is not an end unto itself. Rather, it is a very effective means to many management ends—be they quantitative or qualitative.

Thus the term management information system (MIS) more aptly defines those portions of financial records that can be used to help run the firm. A good MIS can quantitatively measure your operation, but it cannot make decisions for you. Rather, the numbers do provide the easiest, quickest, and best early warning indicator of how a management system is doing—whatever its goals. How that information is used is entirely up to the people in control of these goals.

To understand what financial management information can mean to a design firm, it is first necessary to understand what it is not:

1 **An MIS is not bookkeeping.**   The books that must be kept by a bookkeeper in every organization simply record the transactions of the firm—where funds came from and where they were spent. A bookkeeper's ledgers per se are of virtually no value as management information. A bookkeeper can be asked to pre-

pare MIS reports from the books, but they would add to, rather than replace, the required records of the books themselves.

2 **An MIS is not accounting.** The role of an accountant, functionally (and professionally for a CPA) is to paint a historical picture of past events, rendered on a basis consistent with standard accounting principles, which allow one business to be compared to another. Such a picture is useful only if your organization's goals are similar to those of a standard business, which is not the case for many design firms. Nor is an accountant generally qualified or willing to tell you how to manage the future. You will be told that you are losing money or that your overhead is 47.6% of your payroll, but unless the accountant is a specialist in design firms you should not expect advice on how to reduce the loss or whether your overhead ratio is too high or too low.

Thus the first requirement for an adequate management information system in your practice is to have someone at management level in charge of reading the numbers. This person must know what reports are needed to help manage the firm and must understand what actions to take (suggest) when the numbers show something is not working according to plan.

This chapter discusses the management information reports that are most useful to the operation of a design firm. A variety of other financial reports must also be maintained in most design firms for basic record-keeping or tax purposes, and all sorts of underlying systems are needed to yield the MIS reports described here. These are well covered in other books and some manuals issued by the professional societies. This is a book for the manager. It is assumed that once the manager knows what report to ask for, the firm's financial support system (e.g., bookkeeper, accountant, computer consultant) will produce it. (Of course, it is never so simple, but that is the subject of Chapter 12.)

The management information reports most valuable to the architect or engineer in practice fall into the categories listed on the following pages in their general order of importance*.

---

*Many of the printouts used to illustrate this chapter are drawn from the Computer-based Financial Management System (CFMS) developed by the AIA and administered by Harper & Shuman, 68 Moulton Street, Cambridge, Massachusetts 02138. It is one of the most comprehensive systems available for either architects or engineers.

PERSONNEL UTILIZATION REPORT

A personnel time analysis/utilization report is the best single indicator of organization productivity. Since design practice is people intensive, with payroll accounting for 55–65% of operating expense in typical firms, the amount of time devoted to billable project activities as compared to overhead activities can highlight in one stroke such key factors as: overstaffing; understaffing; efficient/inefficient project management (managers); efficient/inefficient department management; and individual underwork/overwork. A time analysis utilization report suitable for the firm's management purposes is shown in Figure 1.

What to read from this report:

1   The ratio is the key indicator. Once some experimental data are gathered, a base ratio for the firm at the target profitability can be established. (In architectural firms 65% productivity (based on total personnel) generally seems to be a breakeven point. In engineering firms it is often about 70%.) A rise in the ratio over several months would indicate growing efficiency. At a certain point it would suggest that the organization may be overworked and may need more people. Conversely, a dropping ratio may signal the need to reduce staff. Perhaps the most valuable use of the firmwide ratio is in times of growth or shrinkage of staff. If 5 or 10 people are added (or cut) and the monthly ratio stays at or near the target, management can assume that the change is being efficiently absorbed. If the ratio drops sharply, however, individual performance should be examined to identify nonproductive employees.

2   Individual utilization rates for each employee are part of the report. It is possible—and advisable—to specify appropriate utilization rates for each class of job in the firm (e.g., draftspersons, 90%; project managers, 75%; specification typists, 35% or whatever. New (and promoted) employees can be advised of the expected utilization rates in their position and be asked to seek additional assignments if they find themselves working below target. It is then further possible to budget or monitor the utilization of each employee. Sharp changes in a person's ratio can be an important indicator of areas where performance reviews are appropriate.

ANDERSON BABCOCK & CROWLEY
ARCHITECTS

TIME ANALYSIS
FOR THE PERIOD 3/16/77-3/31/77

DP CL EMPLOYEE		TOTAL HRS WKD	TOTAL DIRECT	TOTAL INDRCT	CHRG RATIO A	B	C	D	VACATN	SICK	HOLDAY	PROMTN	INDIRECT TIME (HRS) CIVIC	MGMT	PROF	STAND	GENRL	COMP	OTHER
A 2 GRAY	C	100	62	38	62	91	71	70	24	8									6
	Y	550	385	165	70	78	74	70	40	8		40					39		30
A 2 STONE	C	110	80	30	73	73	92	75				30							6
	Y	580	464	116	80	80	89	75				100	16						30
A 2 LAMBERT	C	80	40	40	50	77	50	65	20	12					12			8	
	Y	480	288	192	60	65	60	65	40		8			104	12		40	24-	
CLASS SUBTOTAL	C	290	182	108	63	79	72	70	44	8		30			12			8	6
	Y	1610	1137	473	71	75	75	70	80	20	16	140	16	104	12		79	24-	30
DEPT SUBTOTAL	C	290	182	108	63	79	72	70	44	8		30			12			8	6
	Y	1610	1137	473	71	75	75	70	80	20	16	140	16	104	12		79	24-	30
FIRMWIDE TOTAL	C	290	182	108	63	79	72	70	44	8		30			12			8	6
	Y	1610	1137	473	71	75	75	70	80	20	16	140	16	104	12		79	24-	30

EXPLANATION OF CHARGEABLE RATIOS:

A = TOTAL DIRECT/TOTAL HRS WKD

B = TOTAL DIRECT/(TOTAL HRS WKD - BENEFIT HOURS)

C = TOTAL DIRECT/STANDARD HOURS

D = TARGET

Figure 1   Personnel Utilization Report.

95

PROJECT PROGRESS REPORT

Detailed budgeting and expense monitoring is the best place to manage the projects of the firm. Obviously, if every project is budgeted profitably , and all are meeting their budgets, the firm will be doing well. But it is never that simple. In firms with 50 to 100 active jobs the MIS printouts alone take considerable time just to read, and monitoring each project manager to keep on top of each project would take far more top management time than is available or necessary.

The solution is twofold:

1 Most individual project budgeting and monitoring should be delegated, making project managers and their intermediate supervisor responsible for the planning and tracking of each job.

2 Top management should concern itself with receiving reports of the exceptions—projects that are missing their targets by significant margins.

To accomplish this, projects should first be budgeted by the responsible project manager (with approval of management) and entered in the MIS system. Then *at the end of each pay period each project manager should be required to estimate the percentage of completion of their jobs* and enter this information with the time cards. (This single input is the keystone of the top management monitor report—see below.) The primary copy of subsequent Project Progress Reports should then go to the assigned project manager who should be responsible to initiate action needed to keep projects on budget (or rebudget when appropriate).

In budgeting projects, do not be confused by the fact that your contract with your client may be cost-plus, or time-and-materials and not subject to a budget. You still can—and should—budget every job internally so your staff is always working to a plan.

With project budgeting and monitoring properly delegated, top management can focus their attention on problem areas. A good MIS identifies these problems in a composite Project Summary Report (Figure 2) and an Office Earnings Report (Figure 3).

What to read from these reports:

1 The most helpful indicator is the variance between the project manager's reported percent complete and the percent actually

ANDERSON, BABCOCK & CROWLEY
ARCHITECTS

PROJECT SUMMARY REPORT
FOR THE PERIOD 3/01/77-3/31/77

PROJECT NUMBER	NAME	SPENT THIS PERIOD HOURS	SPENT THIS PERIOD DOLLARS	SPENT TO DATE HOURS	SPENT TO DATE DOLLARS	TOTAL BUDGET HOURS	TOTAL BUDGET DOLLARS	PCT EXP	COMPL RPT	BALANCE REMAINING HOURS	BALANCE REMAINING DOLLARS
95.00	MISC JOBS										
98.00	PERSONAL SERVICES		849		1009						1009-
1000.00	COMPLETED JOBS			14600	462578		164752	280	100	7500-	297826-
1005.00	CITY HALL	490	15812	1760	76901	7500	272660	28	27	4798-	195759-
1019.00	BALBOA	64	482	4229	79333	4138	79020	100	97	8-	313-
1023.00	ABC PLAZA		9	116	4770	170	7534	63	59	69	2764
1025.00	J L SMITH HOME			45	1303	165	5690	23	22	110	4387
1027.00	CITY HALL LOBBY			30	1495	100	4666	32	33	79	3171
1028.00	CITY HALL AC	75	1745	1167	34843	950	33670	103	80	29-	1173-
1030.00	AJAX FACTORY	232	2715	1444	30429	1310	33614	91	69	80	3185
1031.00	PROJECT Y		273	865	16520	667	13936	118	99	65-	2584-
1033.00	DANCE CENTER		142	401	7937	1930	33362	24	21	635	25425
1034.00	GOVERNMENT CENTER	223	4014	1928	43752	2182	55834	78	65	300	12091
1035.00	WGH ELEMENTARY SCHOOL	98	2075	1320	35912	3210	54502	66	55	465	18590
1036.00	111 BEACON STREET	267	3011	1615	35998	2655	57301	63	51	532	21303
1037.00	FOREST HILLS	113	1389	527	14117	954	21382	66	54	182	7265
1038.00	KLH OFFICE		1	397	13448	1060	18821	71	86	134	5373
1039.00	UN WISC LIBRARY	255	7272	2305	116934	3960	93324	125	98	590-	23610-
1040.00	GNH MUSIC HALL	76	1652	996	37758	855	69569	54	47	800	31811
1041.00	LANDOWER MEMORIAL		1596	884	26152	690	17509	149	99	216-	8643-
1042.00	BRUNSWICK PLANT	201	1805	1447	16997	3759	20241	84	59	81	3244
1043.00	MOBIL WAREHOUSE	389	5889		31450		144669	22	14	2830	113219
1044.97	MOLINE BUS DEPOT	16									
1046.00	VA HOSPITAL	53	455	55	1428	250	4034	35		65	2606
1047.00	CENTER PLAZA	492	5815	1289	25349	525	63681	40		956	38332
1048.00	SOUTH HIGH SCHOOL	10	141	10	309		168	184		4-	141-
	TOTALS	3054	57153	37448	1116731	37030	1269949	88	56	3604	153218

Figure 2 Project Summary Report.

expended, as shown in the Project Summary Report (Figure 2). When the percent reported is more than, say, 5% below the actual expended, it is time for top management to take a look and keep watch. It is also possible to flag any project on the Office Earnings Report when the loss for the project or the year to date exceeds a certain amount—say $2,500. To make this identification easy, the bookkeeping group can be instructed to mark in red the MIS printouts before they are presented to the top manager. Or the key information can be taken off and presented in a summary:

Troubled Project Report

Project Name	Estimated % Complete	% Expended	Loss to Date	Total Compensation
A	65	73	4,000	20,000
B	10	17	12,000	100,000
Etc.				

2   The bottom line of the Office Earnings Report tracks progress toward budgeted profitability. This information, with the percentage calculated manually, goes directly to the Executive Summary Report (see below) as follows:

Project Revenue Earned Year to date	Spent Year to date	Net Income (Loss)	Profit (%)
213,452	189,305	24,148	13%

When profitability begins to fall below targets, it is possible to directly identify projects that have caused it.

In summary, to keep a design firm efficient and profitable projects must be managed efficiently and profitably. This cannot be done from the top down in a firm of any size. Rather, responsibility for project performance must be felt (delegated) from the bottom up. Top management's job is then to manage the exceptions.

ANDERSON, BABCOCK & CROWLEY
ARCHITECTS

OFFICE EARNING REPORT
AS OF 3/31/77

NUMBER	PROJECT NAME	COMP	PCT COMPT	PROJECT TO DATE — EARNED INCOME	BILLED	UNBILLED SERVICES	RECEIVED	A/R	SPENT	PROFIT (LOSS)	YEAR TO DATE — EARNED	SPENT	PROFIT (LOSS)
95.00	MISC JOBS												
98.00	PERSONAL SERVICES		3	1420	1420		1433	13-	1009	410	1420	1009	410
1000.00	COMPLETED JOBS	483932	4	483932	483732	200	481732	2000	462578	21353		1346	1346-
1005.00	CITY HALL	336325	27	89767	89767		73344	16423	76901	12866	46000	40000	6000
1019.00	BALBOA	100000	94	90000	73485	16515	28053	45432	79333	10667		4692	4692-
1023.00	ABC PLAZA	7500	58	5540	5540		5540		4770	769	791	552	238
1025.00	J L SMITH HOME	5000	21	1471		1471		1500	1303	168	184-		184-
1027.00	CITY HALL LOBBY	16000	32	3020	3020		3020		1495	1525			
1028.00	CITY HALL AC	28800	79	22901	22901		10391	12509	34843	11942-	10040	13673	3633-
1030.00	AJAX FACTORY		69	24000	28800	4800-	25000	3800	30429	6429-	4007	11733	7726-
1031.00	PROJECT Y	10300	99	10300	10300		10300		16520	6220-		1962	1962-
1033.00	DANCE CENTER	28000	21	6772	6772		5017	1755	7937	1164-	702	1232	529-
1034.00	GOVERNMENT CENTER	55000	64	52800	52800		41800	11000	43752	9047	16600	12250	4349
1035.00	WGH ELEMENTARY SCHOOL	53200	53	54569	54569		37489	17080	35912	18656	18756	4463	14293
1036.00	111 BEACON STREET	68000	48	48960	48960		42160	6800	35998	12961	13689	11328	2360
1037.00	FOREST HILLS	20000	53	13500	13500		12000	1500	14117	617-	2519	3763	1244-
1038.00	KLH OFFICE	16000	84	14761	14761		14761		13448	1313	792	665	127
1039.00	UN WISC LIBRARY	100000	98	132862	132862		72991	59871	116934	15928	5133	1349	3784
1040.00	GNH MUSIC HALL	100000	47	56855	56855		31865	24989	37758	19096	10115	11194	1079-
1041.00	LANDOWER MEMORIAL	20000	99	34793	34793		19332	15461	26152	8641	14793	13230	1563
1042.00	BRUNSWICK PLANT	18000	58	22872	22872		13425	9446	16997	5874	12143	8965	3177
1043.00	MOBIL WAREHOUSE	79075	7	32718	32718		22909	9808	31450	1267	20858	18803	2054
1044.97	MOLINE BUS DEPOT		0										
1046.00	VA HOSPITAL	7000	4	2795	2795			2795	1428	1366	2795	1428	1366
1047.00	CENTER PLAZA	112000	4	32480	32480			32480	25349	7130	32480	25349	7130
1048.00	SOUTH HIGH SCHOOL	10000	4						309	309-		309	309-
	TOTALS	1684132		1239092	1225706	13386	937805	287902	1116731	122361	213452	189305	24148

Figure 3   Office Earnings Report.

99

WORKLOAD FORECASTS

There is no easy, efficient way to forecast workload in a design firm. It would be ideal to be able to add up the person-weeks required to do all the work in the firm, month by month, and thereby know whether to add or reduce staff, accelerate or stretch out work. But in a firm of 10 to 15 or more people detailed projections of the personnel time required to service every project are subject to so many variables that the process is not worth the effort.

The solution lies in forecasting on a macro- rather than microscale. This involves working directly from forecasts of earnings. If each project manager is asked to project the fee to be earned on his or her projects for 3 to 6 months ahead, these projections can be totaled to produce a gross earnings forecast, as in Figure 4.

This forecast can then be translated into a manpower projection by using the firm's experience factor for gross earnings per month per person. (For example, in 1980 dollars the range might be $4000 to $4500 per month per total personnel; or $5000 to $5500 per technical person. Each firm must calculate its own actual numbers.) Once this information is known, the earnings projection can be converted to staff projection as follows:

Projected Earnings	Forecast Total Staff Required at $4,500	Forecast Technical Staff Required at $5,500
Month 1: $89,900	20	16
Month 2: $111,800	25	20
Month 3: $64,400	14	12

What to read from this report:

1   The obvious use of the report is in projecting staff needs. But the projections should not be taken literally. By comparing actual month-to-month earnings with the forecast, helpful experience in discounting the variables can be gained.

2   The forecast can also identify aberrations in the projected workload. When the projections show a fairly steady trend, they probably are reliable. When they show wide swings, however (experience will determine how wide is "wide"), they can alert top management to go back into the detail and find the cause.

ABC DESIGN ASSOCIATES

WORKLOAD FORECAST

PROJECT	FUTURE MONTH 1	FUTURE MONTH 2	FUTURE MONTH 3
HOTEL 40870 REMAINING FEE	5100	5100	5100
HOTEL BRIDGE 17.70 REMAINING FEE	—	300	400
BANK BUILDING 33420 REMAINING FEE	4000	4000	4000
4TH AVE EXPANSION (HOURLY RATE)	5000	3000	3000
SYSTEM 54000 REMAINING FEE	3000	10000	10000
INDUSTRY. PHASE I 360000 REMAINING FEE	32000	40000	60000
CONDOMINIUM ARCHITECTURE	25000	17000	—
STRUCTURAL	9000	8000	—
M & E	6000	4200	600
REROOF (TIME AND MATERIALS)	800	700	1300
TOTALS	89900	111800	64000

Figure 4 Workload Forecast.

ACCRUAL EARNINGS STATEMENT

The bottom line measurement of month-to-month firm performance is an Income Expense Statement prepared on a "quick" accrual basis. This means that revenue is recorded as earned, not as cash received. Expenses generally can be recorded on a cash basis if payroll and overhead expenses are current. The only major expense that must be separately accrued to prepare a quick statement is consultant expense related to that month's revenue. An accrual earnings statement is illustrated in Figure 5.

What to read from this report:

1   The bottom line gives the profit for the month and the year to date and calculates the profit as a percent of gross income. This immediately shows how you are doing.

2   The firm's overhead ratio is calculated directly from the statement by division:

$$\frac{\text{Total Indirect Expense}}{\text{Direct salary expense}} \div \begin{array}{c} \text{This Month} \\ \dfrac{20{,}663}{19{,}995} = 103 \end{array} \qquad \begin{array}{c} \text{Year to Date} \\ \dfrac{69{,}611}{58{,}344} = 119 \end{array}$$

The importance of monitoring the overhead ratio lies in its ability to quickly alert management whenever the trend becomes adverse to the budget (or history).

3   The firm's actual billing multiple can be calculated by division:

$$\frac{\text{Fee Income}}{\text{Direct labor}} \div \begin{array}{c} \text{This Month} \\ \dfrac{60{,}000}{19{,}995} = 3.0 \end{array} \qquad \begin{array}{c} \text{Year to Date} \\ \dfrac{210{,}000}{58{,}344} = 3.6 \end{array}$$

It is possible, especially in inflationary times, to be managing all operations efficiently, but to have profitability drop because the firm underprices its work. A declining trend in the billing multiple can alert management to the need to revise its prices. [Note: The multiple calculated here is not directly comparable to a typical contract multiplier (e.g., 2.5 times direct personnel expense) because it is calculated on direct labor without the benefit expense factor added.

ANDERSON, BABCOCK & CROWLEY
ARCHITECTS

INCOME/EXPENSE STATEMENT
FOR THE PERIOD 3/01/77-3/31/77

	------------------------ INCOME ------------------------			--PERCENT OF TOTAL INCOME--	
ACCT NO	NAME OF ACCOUNT	THIS PERIOD	YEAR TO DATE	THIS PERIOD	YEAR TO DATE
401.00	BILLED FEE INCOME	60000.00	210000.00	90.2	98.4
404.00	UNBILLED INCOME	6211.07	2052.73	9.3	1.0
	SUBTOTAL	66211.07	212052.73	99.5	99.4
499.00	REIMBURSABLE INCOME	300.00	1400.00	0.5	0.6
	SUBTOTAL	300.00	1400.00	0.5	0.6
	TOTAL INCOME	66511.07	213452.73	100.00	100.00

	------------------ REIMBURSABLE EXPENSES ------------------			--PERCENT OF TOTAL INCOME--	
ACCT NO	NAME OF ACCOUNT	THIS PERIOD	YEAR TO DATE	THIS PERIOD	YEAR TO DATE
516.00	TRAVEL	100.00	500.00	0.2	0.2
517.00	REPRODUCTIONS	200.00	1000.00	0.3	0.4
	SUBTOTAL	300.00	1500.00	0.5	.7
	TOTAL REIMBURSABLE EXPENSE	300.00	1500.00	0.5	.7

	-------------------- DIRECT EXPENSE --------------------			--PERCENT OF TOTAL INCOME--	
ACCT NO	NAME OF ACCOUNT	THIS PERIOD	YEAR TO DATE	THIS PERIOD	YEAR TO DATE
602.00	DIRECT LABOR	19995.78	58344.84	30.0	27.3
604.00	TEMPORARY HELP	39.20	333.20	.1	0.2
	SUBTOTAL	20034.98	58678.04	30.1	27.5
	TOTAL DIRECT EXPENSE	41322.28	118193.93	62.1	55.4

	-------------------- INDIRECT EXPENSE --------------------			--PERCENT OF TOTAL INCOME--	
ACCT NO	NAME OF ACCOUNT	THIS PERIOD	YEAR TO DATE	THIS PERIOD	YEAR TO DATE
702.00	INDIRECT LABOR	9818.53	29334.90	14.8	13.7
703.00	JOB COST VARIANCE	292.50	963.38	0.4	.5
	SUBTOTAL	10111.03	30298.28	15.2	14.2
711.00	EMPLOYER'S FICA TAX	5400.00	18000.00	8.1	8.4
	TOTAL INDIRECT EXPENSE	20663.64	69611.08	31.1	32.6
	TOTAL EXPENSES	62285.92	189305.01	93.6	88.7
	PROFIT/LOSS	4225.15	24147.72	6.4	11.3

Figure 5   Accrual Earnings Statement.

ACCRUAL BALANCE SHEET

An accrual balance sheet (Figure 6) is not a day-to-day management tool, and many firms look at it only at quarterly or semiannual intervals. Nevertheless, it does have two important uses.

What to read from this report:

1   The accrual net worth describes the firm's financial worth. This has uses in evaluing ownership changes, decisions on major investments, and so on.
2   The accrual balance sheet (assuming it is healthy) is the best tool to show to the firm's bankers whenever it is necessary to borrow money.

```
                    ANDERSON, BABCOCK & CROWLEY
                            ARCHITECTS

                           BALANCE SHEET
                           AS OF 3/31/77


    ---------------------- ASSETS -----------------------------

    ACCT NO   NAME OF ACCOUNT                     AMOUNT

    101.00    CHECKING ACCOUNT                  54059.67
    102.00    SAVINGS ACCOUNT                    4340.85
    103.00    PETTY CASH                           50.00
              SUBTOTAL                          58450.52

    111.00    ACCTS RECEIVABLE-CLIENTS         287902.21
    113.00    ACCTS RECEIVABLE-OTHER             1171.90
    115.00    TRAVEL ADVANCES                    2453.98
              SUBTOTAL                         291528.09

    121.00    UNBILLED SERVICES                 13386.00
              SUBTOTAL                          13386.00

    131.00    FURNITURE AND FIXTURES            50000.00
    132.00    RESERVE FOR DEPR. F & F            8951.46-
              SUBTOTAL                          41048.54


              TOTAL ASSETS                     404413.15

    ------------- LIABILITIES AND NET WORTH ------------

    ACCT NO   NAME OF ACCOUNT                     AMOUNT

    201.00    NOTES PAYABLE-CURRENT             50000.00
              SUBTOTAL                          50000.00

    211.00    ACCOUNTS PAYABLE-CONSULT.         58477.30
              SUBTOTAL                          58477.30

    231.00    SALARIES PAYABLE                      0.00
    232.00    FICA WITHHOLDING                      0.00
    233.00    FEDERAL WITHHOLDING                   0.00
    234.00    STATE WITHHOLDING                     0.00
    235.00    OTHER WITHHOLDING                     0.00
              SUBTOTAL                              0.00

              TOTAL LIABILITIES                108477.30


    300.00    CAPITAL STOCK                     67595.00
    301.00    PAID IN SURPLUS                  110925.00
    302.00    RETAINED EARNINGS-CURR            24147.72
    303.00    RETAINED EARNINGS-PRIOR           93268.13
              SUBTOTAL                         295935.85

              TOTAL NET WORTH                  295935.85

              TOTAL LIABILITIES AND NET WORTH  404413.15
```

Figure 6   Accrual Balance Sheet.

CASH MANAGEMENT REPORT

There is an important distinction between cash management and accrual management, and that difference must be kept in mind to avoid mismanaging the firm. The accrual earnings statements are the true reflection of the firm's performance. If profits are accruing (and the clients are solvent) the firm is healthy, regardless of its cash position. Cash itself may fluctuate widely at different times of the year depending on the rate of collections, and to make major management decisions based on the cash balance in the bank accounts can result in serious mistakes. For example, the firm can be flush with cash while losing money on an accrual basis. If economies are delayed because of the availability of cash, past profits may be wasted. Conversely, the firm may be very short of cash during a highly profitable growth period. Avoiding additional expenditures to support that growth because of lack of cash would waste the opportunity. (Bank loans solve temporary cash shortages if you can show the banker a healthy accrual statement.) Thus a Cash Management Report (Figure 7) is intended to help manage cash—not to help manage the firm.

What to read from this report:

1   The primary value of the report lies in alerting management to:
    (a) When to press for faster collections from clients to avoid borrowing.
    (b) When to delay payments to suppliers and consultants to conserve cash and avoid borrowing.
    (c) When to borrow bank money to cover a shortfall.
2   A very important auxiliary use of the cash management report is in income tax planning. Since most design organizations keep cash basis accounts for tax purposes, as differentiated from the accrual basis on which they are managed (see below), it becomes important toward the end of the year to control the amount of cash on hand. This is accomplished by specially managing the way accounts are billed and collected.

ABC DESIGN ASSOCIATES

CASH MANAGEMENT REPORT

	LAST MONTH ACTUAL	THIS MONTH PROJECTED	THIS MONTH ACTUAL	NEXT MONTH PROJECTED	NEXT MONTH ACTUAL
BEGINNING CASH POSITION	29371	58499		30499	
CASH RECEIPTS	103500	47000		85000	
CASH EXPENSE	74372	75000		75000	
ENDING CASH POSITION	58499	30499		40499	

	TOTAL	CURRENT	30-60 DAYS	60-90 DAYS	MORE THAN 90 DAYS
ACCOUNTS RECEIVABLE	287902	105654	75468	44700	62080
ACCOUNTS PAYABLE ON HAND	58477	43195	15282		

Figure 7 Cash Management Report.

AGING SCHEDULE OF RECEIVABLES

The schedule of Aged Accounts Receivable (Figure 8) is management's most useful tool to monitor cash intake and also is a valuable indicator of client satisfaction and/or solvency. It is also one of the simplest reports to prepare, even in a small firm.

In practice, the schedule of accounts receivable is most valid if the firm bills all or most of its clients monthly, as work is performed. Although there are some clients who still insist on paying by phases, the great majority of design firms today are writing their contracts to provide for monthly billings, and they should expect prompt payment. The aging schedule, therefore highlights those projects and clients where payment is not being received according to plan (or contract).

What to read from this report:

1   The first use of the schedule is to signal when action should be taken to collect what is owed the firm. There should be a firm policy calling for mandatory action when an account becomes overdue—at most 45 to 60 days after billing. The usual procedures include typing a special letter to the client for partner signature; or requiring a partner/project manager to phone the client; or even notifying the client that work is being stopped until payment is received. The exact nature and sequence of actions will depend on the type of clients, and the nature of the firm. The essential point is that there should be standard collection procedures triggered by the aging schedule.

2   A secondary but important benefit of the schedule is its ability to signal client trouble. Most clients pay their bills with reasonable promptness. When a "regular" client suddenly lets bills slide 90 days or more, it may be a sign of dissatisfaction with the design firm's performance, or may signal some basic change in the client's financial position. Whatever the case, top management should contact every client with bills outstanding over 90 days and try to find the cause.

ANDERSON, BABCOCK & CROWLEY
ARCHITECTS

AGED ACCOUNTS RECEIVABLE
AS OF 3/31/77

PROJECT NUMBER	PROJECT/PRINCIPAL	INVOICE NUMBER	DATE	TOTAL	CURRENT	30-60	60-90	90-120	120-150	OVER 150
00098.00	PERSONAL SERVICES BABCOCK	00199	03/01/77	13.12-	13.12-					
01000.00	COMPLETED JOBS BABCOCK	00067	08/31/76							1,999.84
01005.00	CITY HALL SMITH	00111	09/30/76	1,063.53					1,063.53	
		00132	11/30/76	5,998.72				5,998.72		
		00166	01/31/77	5,165.75		5,165.75				
		00187	03/28/77	4,195.87	4,195.87					
		TOTALS		16,423.87	4,195.87	5,165.75		5,998.72	1,063.53	
• • •										
	TOTALS			287,902.21	35,654.92	75,468.20	24700.00	65,324.26	1,063.53	85,691.30

Figure 8   Aged Accounts Receivable.

109

PROFIT-PLANNING MONITOR

It is excellent practice to budget income and expenses a year in advance. Monitoring that budget, then, is a convenient way to keep on top of the variances that inevitably occur as the year progresses. For most budget items it is sufficient to use annual budgeting and to calculate monthly progress on a straight-line $1/12$ th basis (Figure 9). Management can easily recognize cases where this is out of line (as in liability insurance which may all be paid in 1 or 2 months).

A separate aspect of the budgeting process for firms involved in work with the Federal government is the need to carefully account for overhead items so that a minimum of costs are disallowed in the contract auditing process. There are a number of legitimate expenses which the government will not allow if they appear on the books in accounts with certain titles (especially in the business development area). Firms doing Federal work need to be specially careful how they set up and keep budget accounts on their MIS.

What to read from this report:

1   Identifying the major variances (say, $10-20\%$) can reveal both overexpenses and underexpenses. If an item is over budget by a large amount, management should have a reason for it or take action to correct it.
2   If an item is far under budget it may indicate an area that is being neglected (e.g., indirect promotion) and needs to be pushed.

ANDERSON, BABCOCK, & CROWLEY
ARCHITECTS

PROFIT PLANNING MONITOR
FOR THE PERIOD 3/1/77 - 3/31/77

ACCOUNT NUMBER	NAME	CURRENT PERIOD				YEAR TO DATE				ANNUAL PLAN
		ACTUAL	PLAN	VARIANCE	PCT	ACTUAL	PLAN	VARIANCE	PCT	
- - - I N C O M E - - -										
401.00	BILLED FEE INCOME	60,000	66,666	6,666-	10-%	210,000	200,000	10,000	5 %	800,000
404.00	UNBILLED INCOME	6,211	4,166	2,044	49	2,052	12,500	10,447-	83-	50,000
	SUBTOTAL	66,211	70,833	4,622-	7-	212,052	212,500	447-	0	850,000
499.00	REIMBURSABLE INCOME	300	833	533-	64-	1,400	2,500	1,100-	44-	10,000
	SUBTOTAL	300	833	533-	64-	1,400	2,500	1,100-	44-	10,000
	TOTAL INCOME	66,511	71,666	5,155-	7-	213,452	215,000	1,547-	1-	860,000
- - REIMBURSABLE EXPENSES - -										
516.00	TRAVEL	100	166	66-	40-%	500	500	0	0 %	2,000
517.00	REPRODUCTIONS	200	500	300-	60-	1,000	1,500	500-	33-	6,000
	SUBTOTAL	300	666	366-	55-	1,500	2,000	500-	25-	8,000
	TOTAL REIMBURSABLE EXPENSE	300	666	366-	55-	1,500	2,000	500-	25-	8,000
- - DIRECT EXPENSE - -										
602.00	DIRECT LABOR	19,995	18,333	1,662	9 %	58,344	55,000	3,344	6 %	220,000
604.00	TEMPORARY HELP	39	83	44-	53-	333	250	83	3	1,000
	SUBTOTAL	20,034	18,416	1,618	8	58,678	55,250	3,428	6	221,000
	TOTAL DIRECT EXPENSE	41,322	40,000	1,322	3	118,193	116,000	2,193	2	416,000
- - INDIRECT EXPENSES - -										
702.00	INDIRECT LABOR	9,818	10,000	181-	2-%	29,334	30,000	665-	2-%	120,000
703.00	JOB COST VARIANCE	292	333	40-	12-	963	1,000	36-	4-	4,000
	SUBTOTAL	10,111	10,333	222-	2-	30,298	31,000	701-	2-	124,000
711.00	EMPLOYER'S FICA TAX	5,400	5,400	0	0	18,000	17,000	1,000	6	50,000
	TOTAL INDIRECT EXPENSE	20,663	26,000	5,336-	20-	69,611	62,600	7,011	11	264,000
	TOTAL EXPENSES	62,285	66,666	4,380-	7-	189,305	180,600	8,705	5	688,000
	PROFIT/LOSS (-)	4,225	5,000	774-	15-	24,148	34,400	10,252-	30	172,000

Figure 9 Profit-Planning Monitor.

EXECUTIVE SUMMARY REPORT

Experience indicates that the easiest way to ensure that financial information will be ignored in a design firm is to distribute too much of it. An
inch-thick computer printout can be a complete turnoff for a busy design
professional whose primary concern is the clients of the moment. Thus
although the foregoing reports are the minimum the firm's financial
manager should be looking at, other principals in the firm generally need
(want) to see a much simpler extraction of highlights.

Such a summary (Figure 10) can be produced from the reports just
described and then distributed to every principal of the firm each month.
Detailed reports may then be distributed regularly only to those who
request them.)

The summary itself can be prepared by the firm's bookkeeper or
controller. The interpretive notes would be added by the financial management principal before the report is distributed.

ABC DESIGN ASSOCIATES
EXECUTIVE SUMMARY OF OPERATIONS

MANAGEMENT INFORMATION SYSTEM HIGHLIGHTS FOR THE PERIOD _____ TO _____

CONTROL ITEM	CURRENT PERIOD	PREVIOUS PERIOD	YEAR TO DATE	TREND	NOTES
NET FEES EARNED	66211	84712	212052	DOWN	ON PLAN TO DATE
PROFIT	4225 (6.4%)	11607 (13.7%)	24148 (11.3%)	DOWN	ON PLAN TO DATE
STAFF UTILIZATION	63	68	71	DOWN	VACATIONS HEAVY NOW
OVERHEAD RATE	103	121	119	UP	
BILLING MULTIPLE	3.0	3.8	3.6	OK	ON PLAN
ACCOUNTS RECEIVABLE	287903	301728	NA	DOWN	
CASH ON HAND	58499	29371	NA	UP	MAY NEED TO BORROW BY (MONTH)

MOST TROUBLED PROJECTS	ESTIMATED % COMPLETE	ACTUAL % EXPENDED	LOSS TO DATE
Project A	65%	73%	4000
Project B	10%	17%	12000
Etc.			
(LIST 10 ITEMS OR FEWER)			

Figure 10 Executive Summary Report.

MANAGEMENT INFORMATION VERSUS TAX INFORMATION

In dealing with all the above it should be kept in mind that current United States income tax laws make it desirable for most design firms to report their performance for tax purposes on a *cash basis*, rather than the *accrual basis* of the management information system. There is no conflict in doing this.

Paying taxes on the basis of cash actually in hand allows a design firm to have some control over its tax bill by accelerating or deferring collections and payables at year's end. In practice, most design firms finance their working capital by keeping a large block of accounts receivable uncollected at tax time each year. This practice is both sound business and perfectly proper under the tax laws. However, some accountants, preoccupied with the letter of the tax laws, have frightened design firm principals away from accrual management records by citing an Internal Revenue Service rule against dual bookkeeping. This rule is intended to prevent a kind of tax manipulation that has nothing to do with the way a design firm operates. To comply with this rule, it is only important that a design firm's basic financial books be kept in such a way that it is easy to convert from accrual to cash and vice versa. In fact, the way the books are maintained need never be in conflict with having an accrual-based management information system. Most bookkeepers can make a quick conversion of cash basis records into the accrual management reports recommended here or vice versa.

COMPUTER OR NO COMPUTER?

As mentioned earlier, this chapter does not aim to define the record-keeping procedures or processing systems that are necessary to produce the management information reports described above. There are a number of manuals coming into print* where the serious financial manager can obtain this information. Beyond the design of the systems, however, is the issue of computerization, and a word about that may be helpful.

The decision about whether or not to computerize one's financial systems should, in principle, be made solely on the basis of efficiency. It is theoretically possible for a manual bookkeeping operation to construct all the reports described above. However, doing it quickly, before the data is obsolete, can be costly and even impractical once the firm size exceeds 10 or 12 people and/or involves more than 15 or 30 client billings per month. When the bookkeeping workload reaches beyond these levels, preparation of the management information report is often delayed.

At this juncture it becomes economic to put the records on computer, because of its ability to generate quickly not only the required bookkeeping reports (payroll, billing, etc.) but the management information as well. With the proliferation of computer service bureaus and the advent of small inexpensive, minicomputers for in-house use, computerized record keeping is within reach of smaller firms. Its net efficiency and speed probably makes computerization a good investment in every firm where one full-time bookkeeper begins to need help to get all the work done.

One serious caution must be kept in mind whenever a firm computerizes its records. This is the danger of generating useless and excessive information. The computer can produce literally pounds of paper reports even in a small firm, and unless this output is carefully designed and its distribution carefully controlled from the beginning, key people in the firm tend to begin to ignore the information, thus nullifying the whole advantage of the computer.

It is best to treat the computer output merely as raw material for the bookkeeping department, and to distribute within the organization only those pieces of the output that key people want and will use. Project managers need only the printouts for their projects. Department heads need only utilization reports on their personnel. Many principals may need only the executive summary, and some may ignore even that. Most important of all, unless one principal is seriously committed to understanding the overall numbers and knows how to make use of them to operate the firm, there may be no value in having the reports at all.

The point is that no computer can manage a firm. Excessive computer output can lead to neglect if it is so overwhelming that it is ignored. By all means, mechanize your records as soon as it is efficient to do so,

*Among the best at this writing is *Financial Management for Architects,* by Robert F. Mattox, The American Institute of Architects, 1980.

but only if there are principals within the firm ready to use the output as a management tool. Then, to implement an MIS, the problem is no longer a matter of finding the hardware and/or a service bureau with qualified software; rather, the challenge is to find a system that will do the job.

MAKING USE OF AN MIS

Having all of the foregoing data won't help to operate the firm unless some financial objectives have been set in the first place. Such objectives, which should be part of the firm's basic goals (Chapter 3), can be defined by a very simple equation:

$$\text{income} - \text{expense} = \text{profit}$$

By deciding which element(s) of the equation will be paramount, a firm can establish the framework for all financially based management decisions. For example:

- If the firm chooses to be *income based,* it might focus on marketing and would adjust staff and expenses up or down according to the volume of work obtained. Such a firm might specialize in a narrow market area and would resign itself to adjusting its operations to the ups and down of that market.
- If the firm is *expense based,* it might be committed to maintaining a certain staff size and associated overhead and would strive to adjust income or sacrifice profit to preserve that expense "nut." Such a firm would be inclined to take marginal work to keep the staff together at times when better work is not available. It might also resist growth if the core group chose to remain at a fixed size.
- If a firm is highly *profit based,* it might strive to maximize the spread between income and expense, without particular regard for the source of income or the kind of expense. Such a firm might, for example, encourage turnover of younger people rather than raising salaries to retain more experienced staff.

Most firms, of course, do not have singular financial goals. The area of emphasis varies according to different priorities from time to time. There must, however, be clear agreement on the priority in the equation at any given time. Then the managers of the firm can look at the MIS in each period and know immediately what actions to take to keep on track. Without such focus, the manager will be unable to decide or get agreement on the next course of action.

Thus the bottom line in managing the numbers in a design firm is not the numbers themselves: rather, it is knowing what the numbers mean, so that the firm can be managed toward its professional goals.

FOUR

KEEPING IT GOING

Chapter 9

LEGAL STRUCTURE AND OWNERSHIP PATTERNS

"We're a corporation, but we operate as a partnership."

Stated by dozens of design professionals

The subject of legal structure and ownership patterns in design firms receives far more attention among design firm principals, their lawyers, and accountants than it is worth. This comes about because design firms, when initiating a legal reorganization, often attempt to mix or consolidate the functional organization of the firm and its legal format. It is important to understand the difference between the two.

> The *functional organization,* in this context, is the actual way in which a firm is controlled and operated. The control person or group are those who in fact make the final policy decisions and set the direction of the firm. Whether that control group is legally a "partnership," a "board of directors," an "executive committee," or whatever is irrelevant to the way it will function. The dynamics of the control group in a professional service organization is determined by its method of decision making: by consensus (most common); by majority vote (seldom); or by deferring to a strong-willed s.o.b. (more often than many would like).

> The *legal organization format* of a design firm can be a professional corporation, a business corporation, a partnership, or a proprietorship. In practice, the choice of Legal format should be made solely for tax and liability reasons, and for no other.

If this point can be accepted—that the legal format of an architectural or engineering firm should have little or nothing to do with its functional organization—choosing the legal format is usually quite simple.

INCORPORATION

The primary advantage of conventional incorporation is limited liability: a corporation is liable for business errors, accidents, omissions, and so on, only to the extent of its assets, thereby shielding from attachment the personal resources of stockholders and officers. At this writing, the professional registration laws of most states hold that professional liability goes with the architect's or engineer's seal and is a personal risk obligation that cannot be shielded by any corporate veil. Thus architects and engineers in a number of states are prevented by law from practicing as conventional corporations.

Few professionals argue with the philosophical principle of personal liability for their professional action, but a consequence of being prevented from incorporating is that design professionals have also been prevented from enjoying the tax benefits that can accrue to corporations.

Corporate practice of architecture or engineering, with the attendant limitation of liability, is allowable in a few states. Wherever this is so, it would be an obvious advantage for a design firm to incorporate. However, the professional liability shelter cannot be exported. Any professional work that a corporate practice firm performs in another state must be done under the professional license of the owner(s) who are registered in that state, and the professional liability flows back to the individual(s).

Thus, in reality, only a minor percentage of design firms in the United States were enjoying corporate protection from professional liability at this writing.

The so called professional corporation is a hybrid that most states created in the 1960s and 1970s to give professionals corporate tax advantages, while continuing to exclude them from the shelter of personal liability for professional acts. The trend toward professional incorporation of design firms grew very rapidly in the 1970s, and surveys made at the end of the decade showed that a majority of all design practices had become corporations in the preceding few years. Professional corporations do enjoy shelter from so-called business liability—chiefly suits from suppliers or landlords for nonpayment of bills or rent or personal accident suits by employees or visitors who might trip on the office doorstep. This shelter is not a major consideration in most firms, however, since the nature of architectural and engineering practice does not lead to large vendor debts and injury suits are normally covered by insurance.

Therefore, the only significant advantage of professional incorporation lies in certain aspects of the tax laws which allow corporations to have more elaborate pension plan programs than are available in partnerships or proprietorships. That is, contributions to pension plans can be deducted as a business expense, before taxes, thereby providing a form of "shelter" to profits when earned and deferral of the taxes thereon until the recipients receive the pension payout many years later. At one time these pension plan advantages could be stacked heavily in favor of the owners of the firm, but recent legislation requires that "qualified" (e.g., tax-favorable) pension plans be fairly democratic and cover all employees of the firm.

Generally, only if the principals are in very high tax brackets (in excess of $75,000 per year)—or if the firm is virtually employee owned—is a corporate pension plan a practical tax shelter in larger firms (with more than 50 or 100 staff members). Under the federal pension plan laws in effect in 1980, many larger firms of modest profitability had closed out earlier pension/profit-sharing trusts because of the burden of complying with the new rules and; instead, they were encouraging their employees—and the owners—to provide for their own pensions under provisions of the so-called Individual Retirement Act (IRA). Thus the number of professional corporations actually enjoying the primary benefit of incorporation was still relatively small as of 1980.

PARTNERSHIP OR PROPRIETORSHIP

The primary advantage of the partnership (or proprietorship) legal format for professional design practice is that it most closely parallels the way in which professional design firms actually function. (The proprietorship format is similar to a partnership except that a single individual is the dominant decision maker and sole owner.)

It is in the so-called legal disadvantages of a partnership that it's relevance to professional practice becomes clear. A partnership offers no shelter from liability, but, as noted above, in most states professionals cannot avoid professional liability in any case. Financially, a partnership provides no tax-favorable opportunity to accumulate capital, but professional firms have little need for capital and accumulating it can cause severe problems in ownership transition (see Chapter 11). Finally, a partnership is not permitted to have a tax-sheltered pension plan under the current rules, but, as noted above, many design firms are not in the financial position where such advantages really count.

In concept, a partnership is a legal vehicle for collaboration among peers—and this is exactly what professional design practice is, or ought to be. The partnership format encourages a healthy balance between self-interest and collective interest, as opposed to the corporation, which is essentially an independent third party in concept. In economic terms partnership profits are distributed annually as earned, and it is up to each partner to provide for his or her personal needs from that return. The "value" of the partnership is chiefly the opportunity to work in it. This tends to moderate the "goodwill" one can claim in selling a partnership interest, but as is explained in Chapter 10, attempts to place a high intangible value on design practice are difficult at best. The potential of a partnership to use deferred compensation as a method of paying out "value" (see Chapter 11) makes the partnership format as financially practical as any other.

Although design professionals have tried mightily in recent years to justify the corporate format for other than tax and liability reasons, it is the author's observation that some of the best known, long-lived architectual and engineering practices in the United States continue to be partnerships. In the other learned professions—especially among lawyers and accountants—the partnership format is by far the most common legal structure among successful practices. The reason appears to lie in the functional nature of professional practice. Where two or more principals share control and decision making, a "partnership" in principle exists. Only when that functional dynamic is working so that the firm can operate effectively will the practice thrive. This creates a "partnership," in fact, and to give it a parallel legal form only makes good sense.

HYBRID FORMATS

For a number of tax and legal reasons, design practices also operate under a variety of hybrid legal formats that attempt to bridge some of the differences described above. The most common is a firm organized as a partnership for ownership and professional contracting purposes, which then owns a "drafting corporation" (usually a conventional business corporation) that employs the staff and serves as a subcontractor to do the work. This dual-format organization can provide the corporate tax advantages while preserving the professional contract-taking flexibility of a partnership in different states where the firm may work.

To broaden participatory ownership among employees below the control group level, there are a number of other hybrid variations of both the partnership and professional corporate form.

In partnerships this is usually called associate partnership, in which key personnel below the control group level have a vested interest in profits. Most associate partnerships attempt to avoid legal status so as to shield associate partners from the legal liability while giving them a defined interest in profits. This must be carefully handled legally to ensure the liability shelter is clear.

The corporate alternative is to have minor stockholders. Though legally cleaner, this hybrid format lacks the ego-recognition status that goes with an associate partnership. Many corporate design firms don't like corporate titles and are experimenting with partnership-like terms such as "principal" and "associate principal."

PRIORITIES FOR MAKING A CHOICE

Although the basic reasons for choosing one legal format over another are pragmatic, some functional and personal priorities can be considered to help define the best direction. Two decisions must be made:

1   **Objectives.**   At the outset there must be agreement between:
    (a) The degree to which the firm will be a group of individuals working for a *common good* e.g., an institutional/corporate approach; and
    (b) The degree to which the firm will serve individuals collaborating out of *self-interest* (e.g., a law firm/medical group approach).
    The difference is significant. A self-interested firm will generally be closely held by a small control group. This is true especially in many smaller firms—with up to 50 or 75 people—where most staff members are younger people with no definite career commitments to the firm and a relatively small number of key people will stay with the firm throughout their working life. The institutional or common-good approach is more favored in larger, broadly held firms where all personnel, including the control group, perceive of themselves as employees of the organization and put perpetuation before self-interest. This is the approach in a number of the larger engineering firms.
2   **Structure.**   There must be a clear distinction between three levels of authority.
    (a) Control group.   Policymakers who set the direction and control the firm toward those goals. Since ownership is the medium of control in a self-interested firm, the control group in such firms must always hold a substantial majority or all of the ownership. In a common-good firm, a board of directors might be composed of a minority of owners,

elected by others. In either case, the control group must be defined. In practice, the control group will always function as a partnership, with most policy decisions made by group consensus. Thus the size of the control group is important to the efficient operation of the firm. If the group is allowed to become too large, with many minority partners wanting a voice in every decision, the firm may bog down.

(b) **Key personnel.** High-value staff whose performance contributes substantially to the success and profitability to the firm, but who influence its direction only indirectly. This group may deserve a large share of the profits they help to generate, but would not normally participate in the controlling ownership. In self-interested firms, any share in ownership that such key personnel might have should be less than an aggregate 25% in order to make clear who will run the show. In a common-good firm, this might be a large diverse group that elects the directors and, in effect, holds democratic control.

(c) **Other staff.** Employees who by function, position, and/or professional status deserve special recognition for their roles in the firm may be called associates, but would not normally have ownership in a self-interested firm. In an insitutional practice they might be minor stockholders.

Clear distinctions between those groups is essential to good organizational relationships. If the qualifications and criteria for participation in the control group are not clear, no organization will remain well managed over the long term.

Once the objectives and the structure of the organization have been clarified in terms of the above, the choice of legal format for operation (e.g., partnership vs. corporation) should become obvious, unless modified solely for tax reasons.

This chapter will have served its purpose if it has made a single point: the functional organization of a practice is far more important than the legal suit in which it is cloaked. If the organization is functionally together then it is ipso facto being well managed. There is very little a legal structure or ownership pattern can do to create good management where it does not already exist.

Chapter 10
VALUATION

"Professional service firms are selling only brainpower. They don't have a product—a soup, a widget or a precast unit of some kind—and don't belong in the publicly owned marketplace."

David B. Benham
Chairman
Benham-Blair & Affiliates

For the same reasons stated in the previous chapter about the relative unimportance of the legal format in the effective operation of a design firm, so too are most conventional formulas for valuing business organizations, irrelevant to establishing the value of a design practice.

The whole concept of a design practice having "value" is relatively new. Until the current generation most architects and engineers ended their practice by finishing the projects at hand, collecting whatever was due, paying the final bills, vacating the office, and going off into retirement with whatever net proceeds were left in the till. Only in the present generation have a sizable number of design practices changed hands through acquisition, merger, or internal buy-out where the question of value becomes important.

As a consequence, no standard for the appraisal of a professional practice has yet been accepted. In the 1970s the three leading management consultants working with design firms all had different formulas for arriving at valuations. However, observers who have compared the three approaches find that they frequently lead to very similar conclusions.

This chapter tries to document the major approaches currently in use. None of the opinions expressed should be considered a recommendation for or against any particular formula in valuing any individual practice. Arriving at a final valuation for a design practice is a wholly individual undertaking that can only be accomplished by considering all the facts surrounding the practice itself, the goals of the sellers, and the goals of the buyers. To comprehend the implications, this chapter must be read in conjunction with Chapter 11, Transferring Ownership.

In order to have any real value, a firm must have a a market interested in acquiring that value. In that context, it must be emphasized at the outset that there are two distinctly different markets for the acquisition of design practices: outside and inside. Their objectives are vastly different, hence they tend to choose very different bases of valuation. For example:

> *Outside buyers* normally put up cash or its equivalent to acquire a practice and expect a direct return on that investment. This tends to favor valuation formulas based on a multiple of earnings, since it will be those earnings that must repay the investment. The sellers in such cases are making a one-time transaction and giving up much or all control, hence they frequently seek the highest value.

Inside buyers are most often concerned with securing a continuing role in the firm, rather than with measurable return on investment. And since sellers to inside buyers frequently intend to stay active in the firm, while selling over a period of time, they look at value in both present and future terms. This tends to favor valuations based on a factor of measurable net worth or other easily computed formulas. Compensation agreements can also substantially influence inside-buyer valuation approaches.

The different formulas described below, therefore, are not directly comparable. Their applicability depends greatly on the cirumstances of the transaction for which the value is being established.

MULTIPLE OF EARNINGS

The most common method valuing conventional businesses is by a multiple of earnings. In this approach, if net average earnings of an entity for a reasonable period are determined to be, say, $100,000 a buyer putting up four to eight times those earnings, ($400,000 or $800,000) would expect to recover the investment in 4 to 8 years.

Such formulations work best in valuing publicly held businesses where the accounting of profits and taxes is established on a basis consistent with other companies and where there is a past history of similar buyers receiving similar returns on their investment.

In privately held professional practices, difficulties in applying the muliple of earnings formula begin with the very definition of earnings. Few design firms calculate—or pay taxes on— "profits" in any conventional sense. Net income is distributed as compensation and bonuses or deferred from year to year through cash vs. accrual tax accounting. In addition, closely held firms generally bury considerable compensation in the form of perquisites to the owners—cars, travel, family on the payroll, and so on.

In a multiple of earnings valuation, therefore, the "earnings" that may appear on the firm's books must be "restated" based on "assumed" equitable salaries, "assumed" value of perks, and so on. This is complicated at best, and whimsical at worst in assuming that a firm can continue to function on different compensation/benefit levels, even though those carrots may have been the incentives that made it successful. This also explains why published surveys of design firm profits always highlight the "low profitability" of practice. In fact, design practice became very profitable in the late 1970s, but no survey has yet been concocted to report this on any realistic and comparable basis.

A further complication of the "restated" earnings approach is that the complicated accounting procedure it requires is very difficult to duplicate in restating value year after year. The multiple of earnings approach is therefore less desirable when ownership is going to be traded frequently (as in internal transfers) or when it is the basis of a buy-sell agreement, affecting estate settlement upon the death of an owner. It is very difficult for an heir's executor or accountant to know whether a restated earnings figure is fair or unfair.

Multiple of earnings valuations are most applicable to one-time transactions where the total ownership of the firm is being traded and the buyer will assume control of and be responsible for the future earnings that will produce the return on investment.

There was an active outside market for acquisition of design firms by conglomerate businesses in the late 1960s and early 1970s at which time values to 7 to 10 times earnings were not uncommon. By the late 1970s most of these had proved to be poor deals, because of the mobility of the assets (people) bought in a design firm and the tendency of the best people when "sold out" to go off on their own (see Chapter 11). Thus by the end of the 1970s the acquisition market for design firms was almost exclusively composed of other design firms, buying for expansion. The acquisitions that were publicly reported were in the range of 3 to 5 times earnings, with the majority of sales around 3 or 4 and the higher price being paid only in cases of exceptional expertise or market position.

FACTOR OF GROSS BILLINGS

A variety of formulas have been used to value design firms based on percentage of gross billings. In principle, this is the same approach as a multiple of earnings; a firm earning a 10% profit that is valued at three times earnings could also be valued at 30% of gross billings—the numbers are exactly the same. In practice, however, a percentage of gross billings has the advantage of not requiring an accounting restatement to arrive at a number (provided it is based on accrual, or earned, billings so as to eliminate any year-to-year tax games). Thus the percentage-of-gross-billings approach tends to be fairer to incremental sales and/or estates, *provided,* that all other factors of firm operation are consistent from year to year. That is a very big "provided." It is of course quite possible for a firm to earn a 20% profit one year and lose money the next year on a higher gross.

In reality, the most appropriate application for percentage-of-gross-billings valuations is exactly the same as for multiple-of-earnings formulas—to one-time transactions with a take-over buyer. The advantage of the gross billings formulation in such cases is that it facilitates arriving at a weighted average value where there have been wide swings in billings in just a few years, as in a rapidly growing firm.

FACTORED BOOK VALUE

Book-value approaches to valuing a practice have the advantage of dealing with real worth rather than with some assumptions about future return on investment. Furthermore, book value tends to reflect the cost of being in business, since it is largely made up of the working capital required to stay alive. Book value is also a standard balance sheet number and can generally be established with relative accounting ease.

In looking at the book value of a design firm, it is essential to do so on an accrual basis, where the accounts receivable and work in proces o aggregate 3 to 4 months' billings. This, plus the value of any furniture and fixtures, is the unrealized capital employed in the practice. If the volume of the practice grows substantially, the accounts receivable will grow and so will the accrued book value (provided that there have been no borrowings to finance the expansion). If a firm's volume shrinks, the excess receivables are in due course collected and, generally, taken as compensation by the owners, and again the accrued book value reflects the new scale of the practice.

Thus the most significant advantage of valuations based on book value is that, all other things being equal, they accurately reflect the net cost of being in business, up or down, over time.

The limitation of valuations based on raw book value is that they do not make allowances for profitability, especially when there is an ongoing clientele or expertise in the marketplace that can be expected to provide continuing business. This is called "goodwill," and applying a value to it is the subject of endless debate among design firm appraisers.

One way to add a factor for goodwill to book value is to establish (by evaluating earnings history) a percentage multiplier—say 1.25 × book, or 2.0 × book, or whatever.

Another approach to factoring book value is to calculate the accrual net worth without allowance for federal income taxes. A pretax net worth assumes that whatever the firm would have in the till on liquidation would go to the owners as additional compensation, rather than remaining in the firm and being taxed to become retained earnings. Thus pretax formulation has the effect of increasing the net worth valuation in corporate firms by 30 to 50%.

In practice today, book value is the most common valuation approach used by design firms for internal ownership transfer. This makes sense for all the reasons stated in the chapter that follows, and it makes sense as a tangible measure of the cost of being in business. The majority of these valuations use after-tax book value if the consideration is paid in cash and pretax book value if the consideration is deferred compensation. Any further multiple of value that may be due a founder is most often paid through additional compensation. When all these variations are added together, the average net transfer value of transactions occurring in the late 1970s was between 1.0 and 1.5 times pretax accrued book value.

ROYALTIES

Recently a number of firms have begun experimenting with royalties as a means of placing a premium on book value, especially to reward original founders for the goodwill they have established.

A royalty is generally calculated on the gross billings of the firm, on the principle that the goodwill applies to the ongoing sales rather than the profits derived from them.

Royalties can be applied for a defined term, often on a declining scale, to allow for the diminishing value of efforts of past owners and the increasing value of the efforts of new owners. Thus a royalty formula might look as follows:

A% of gross billings for year 1
B% of gross billings for year 2
C% of gross billings for year 3
D% of gross billings for year 4
Etc.

The value of A through D would depend on the backlog at the time of sale, the ongoing percentage of the firm's business that comes from repeat clients, and the ongoing role, if any, that past owners will continue to play in the firm. Recent royalty agreements, in selected firms have ranged from 2 to 5% at the start, declining in four or five equal increments by ½ to 1% per year. Royalties in this context are considered to be treated for tax purposes as an ordinary expense to the firm, and ordinary income to the recipient, so the negotiated amount would be based on this assumption.

Longer-term royalties can be justified when the name of a founder is going to be continued in the name of the firm. In principle, this could be a rationale even for a perpetual royalty payable to the heirs of a founder. In practice, a recent valuation agreement negotiated in one firm provides for a 2% of gross royalty payable as long as the founder's name is used. The new owners, however, may change the firm's name and eliminate the royalty at any time after 5 years, and the founder may reclaim the name, and forfeit the royalty, if he does not like the image the firm is projecting in his name.

Obviously, many variations are possible in the royalty approach. Its flexibility makes it likely that there will be more and more experimentation with royalty valuations of goodwill in both inside and outside transactions in the years ahead.

The overriding lesson of recent experience with design firm valuations is that the goodwill of a professional practice is a fragile thing. The market itself, in terms of potential buyers, is not large. Buyers are not inclined to pay a high price (over real book value) except for unusual or very large practices. Thus it is not realistic for most design professionals to build their estates around the buy-sell value of their practice. Rather, the time to get rich from architectural or engineering practice is through current compensation while you are in active practice. The way to do that is to be very good at what you do, charge what you are really worth, and manage well so there is plenty to take home.

Chapter 11

TRANSFERRING OWNERSHIP

"In professional organizations where there is no chance for capital accumulation, the founders must pick their successors well if they expect to receive some return on their investment."

Quoted by Norman C. Zimmer, FAIA
Partner
Zimmer-Gunsul-Frasca

Ownership transition became in the 1970s the most commonly discussed, completely misunderstood, and frequently mismanaged aspect of design firm practice. The reasons lie partly in history and partly in the very special nature of the bottom line in design practice, which makes inapplicable much of the conventional wisdom that applies to buying and selling of other kinds of businesses.

In the first place, the question of ownership succession is a relatively new challenge for design firm principals. Until World War II the typical office had one or more registered professionals in striped pants and a staff of draftsmen. When it came time to retire, the principals laid off the staff, collected their receivables, turned the key in the door, and that was it. There are a few notable exceptions—some design firms are as much as 100 years old—but often these have been carried on by sons of the founders.

Since the 1940s, however, the nature of design practice has changed substantially. Firms are larger; multidiscipline practice is common; and, most significantly, the majority of staff personnel are graduate and/or registered professionals. Many of today's successful practices have become organizations, and are worth preserving if continuity can be achieved.

Realizing this objective, though, requires serious business planning, for design practice has several characteristics that impact succession in leadership:

1   Most good designers like to make the final decisions. So long as founders do not delegate or share this responsibility, their best potential successors will leave the firm in their 30s and set up their own shops.

2   When control is concentrated at the top in a design firm, the second line of management usually represents complimentary, not duplicated skills. Handing leadership to that second line is no assurance of success, because they often lack the very skills that made the founders flourish.

At the very least, these hazards say that if you wish to have your organization survive you, you must start planning early. As a rule of thumb, a firm should have a definite plan for succession by the time the founding principals reach 50. The plan should be taking effect—with new leaders given authority as well as responsibility—by the time the founders are 55. Few successful transitions have been accomplished in 5 years or less.

If the goal of a practice is for transition of ownership, a number of guidelines must be understood. It must be emphasized that legal, tax, and accounting considerations are not the critical factors. Design practice is a people business, and no transition plan will work unless it addresses first and foremost the human considerations.

In planning for transition, the founders of a firm generally aim to achieve the following objectives:

1   To retain control as long as possible.
2   To keep peace among their ambitious successors as long as possible.
3   To ensure that the firm they created is perpetuated and avoid the failure of seeing clients lost to competitors.
4   To obtain the maximum value for their equity and to retain their perks and fringe benefits as long as possible.
5   To have a clear picture of their future in the firm after control becomes shared.

These goals may not always be compatible. The goal of maximum economic return, for example, is very difficult to achieve through an inside sale. Few design firms have a second line of management with independent means. If the Juniors are to buy out the seniors they will have to do it with the salaries and bonuses they receive from the firm. Thus owners who want a million dollars from the firm and want their employees to buy them out must give the employees that million with one hand and take it back with the other. Even if this were a good deal, which is doubtful, the tax conseqeunces make it impractical.

If maximum dollars are the goal, the only practical alternative is to sell the firm to outside interests. Several years ago a flurry of acquisitions of architectural and engineering firms by outside conglomerates allowed some founders to cash in handsomely. But the success records of these acquisitions has been very poor. Since good professionals have always preferred to work for themselves, the best younger people in most of the firms that were acquired by outside interests tended to leave and go off on their own rather than work for absentee owners. Many of the firms acquired by third parties in the late 1960s and early 1970s have since been sold back to their employees—or have entirely vanished. As a consequence, the going rate for informed acquisition of design firms has dropped from 7 to 10 times the earnings in the 1969–1972 period to 3 to

5 times the earnings in 1980—and the lower rate can generally be achieved through inside sale. It thus seems clear to most informed observers that the only realistic transition options for the majority of design practices are inside sale to the firm's key people or a true merger, with those key people becoming part of the ownership/control group of the newly combined firms.

In all such transitions, the selling founders will be succesful only if they match their objectives to those of the acquiring generation. Buyers' goals, in contrast to the sellers goals listed above, usually include:

1 Professional status and recognition at about the same age at which the founders put their names on the letterhead.
2 A voice in the control of their destiny as soon as they become owners.
3 A clear picture of when they will assume full control.
4 Acquisition of the practice at a price that is no greater than the risk of walking out and starting their own firm across the street.

When the goals of the inside buyers are paired with those of the sellers, it becomes clear that a successful transition plan must be a compromise between the motives and values of the two parties.

The consequences of avoiding this compromise can be severe. If the sellers wait too long to relinquish some control, they will lose their best successors and will be left with a second team as potential buyers. On the other hand, if they move too early to hand over the reins, the founders may lose the very motivation that makes it fun and worthwhile to stay in practice.

POLICY CONSIDERATIONS

There are no right solutions to the dilemma just described. Each founder/principal must make a choice based on personal career and life goals. The resulting plan for ownership transition, however, should provide a clear policy on the following considerations, listed in the order of their importance:

1 **Control.**   The single most important issue between all sellers and buyers in design practice is control. Ownership distribution

plans that spread ownership widely among employees but don't provide for the divestiture of at least some control may be helpful morale builders but they are not sufficient motivators to ensure the retention of—or top performance from—the best successors. If you are not willing to share some control immediately, at least specify when majority control will come to pass; otherwise, don't call it an "ownership transition" plan. On the other hand, don't be afraid to negotiate the control issue with key successors. Their perception of what constitutes adequate sharing of control is often much more palatable than a nervous founder might expect.

2 **Valuation.** There is a direct correlation between control and value. In a one-time sellout a seller may get more value if willing to relinquish 100% of control immediately. In a long-term buy-in, however, where control is not going to pass, it is difficult to persuade a junior buyer to understand why a premium should be paid when there is no measurable return on his or her investment. "Pay now, get the goods later" has not been the slogan that has made the American economy what it is. The whole subject of valuation is discussed separately in Chapter 10, but it is critical to any ownership transition plan that the valuation set on the transaction be reasonable. In the long run the firm must pay the buyers whatever consideration is involved, so that unrealistic values are self-defeating. Founders who want to milk their firm can do it directly at much less tax cost than by asking their employees to become fatted cows. Design practice can be very profitable in terms of current income, but it is not a place to make great capital gains. Founder/owners who want to get rich from design practice must do so during their working years or through side investments. When it comes time to sell the equity it should be enough to recover the invested net worth (not all founders are able to do even this) plus a reasonable allowance for goodwill only if, in fact, there is goodwill that provides future value to the successors (e.g., substantial client continuity/loyalty that can be attributed to the efforts of the sellers).

3 **Compensation.** As mentioned above, the best way to get rich in design practice is by way of current compensation, rather than through residual equity when the firm is sold. Thus a

sound ownership transition plan must deal clearly with future compensation for both the sellers and the buyers. If all owners are going to have equal compensation (common but not necessarily recommended practice), this must be recognized. If compensation is going to be unequal (the best route), the mechanism for setting compensation, profit sharing, and return on investment must be clearly spelled out at the time of ownership transfer, or the issue will come back to haunt everyone later.

4 **Mechanics.** The plan for buying and selling ownership should include the following stipulations to avoid later misunderstandings:

   (a) Ownership should be limited to active employees of the firm, with outside shareholders—especially the estates of deceased owners—prohibited.

   (b) Buy-sell transactions should always be with or controlled by the firm, not between individual owners. Then as pieces of ownership are either issued or retired, the pro rata weight of the shares of the other owners remains consistent. This also prevents side deals and requires that the full control group participate in all decisions about who will own interests in the firm.

   (c) Ages for divestiture should be specified. Though it is not wise—and may be illegal—to force retirement at a specific age, it is proper to stipulate the age for divestiture of ownership, thereby returning each owner to employee status if they stay on beyond the divestiture age. One of the most successful ownership transitions in a design firm has a simple provision requiring each owner to sell back 20% of his or her interest each year beginning at age 60. This encourages individual owners to start planning early to select their successors as well as for their own future.

   (d) There should be penalties for early withdrawal/retirement. If the purpose of ownership is to encourage retention of key personnel, it makes no sense to help a young leader to buy into the firm, let the value run up, and then allow that person to leave during their midlife crisis, taking the appreciated value along—at the expense of the firm. Depending on how the buy-in mechanism is structured, the agreement should discourage premature withdrawal by providing that anyone who leaves voluntarily before a certain age (say 55) may not receive more for their interest than he or she paid into the firm. After age 55, many firms provide a sliding redemption scale, with the value discounted, for example, by 5% for each year that a person departs before age 60. Thus an owner withdrawing at age 55 might get 25% less (5 years × 5%) than the full value.

(e) Involuntary withdrawal should also be formulated. A partnership/stockholder agreement that does not define the mechanisms by which an owner can be asked to leave is asking for trouble downrange. No marriages—especially professional practice associations—are guaranteed to last a lifetime. A good ownership transition plan must spell out the basis on which an owner can be asked to leave, and must stipulate what will be paid for involuntary withdrawal. Obviously, you can't ask someone to leave and then extract a penalty for early withdrawal. Usually, an excused owner would receive full retirement value, thereby allowing room for individual negotiations when there is some mutuality in a termination/withdrawal.

A COMPOSITE PLAN FOR TRANSFERRING OWNERSHIP

Currently, a large number of approaches to ownership transition are being tried in design firms across the United States. Some are working well—thus far. Others need more time to demonstrate their merit. All must be watched for at least another generation before anyone can be expected to write the definitive book of boiler plate plans for others to copy—if in fact that can ever occur. Meanwhile, whatever is working to achieve the goals of an individual firm should be considered as the state of the art.

For those still struggling to find a plan that works, the following is a composite that has been tried in a number of firms with some success. It rests on certain assumptions that may not apply in all cases. Paramount among these is the use of deferred compensation in lieu of capital gains payout. The applicability of this framework to a firm can be determined only after a careful consideration of the players, roles, and goals involved. But it is presented here to illustrate that there are practical ways in which compromise the different priorities and objectives present in transferring ownership in a design firm.

The composite plan has six elements:

1   Firm valuation for buy-sell transactions among successors is based at or near the pretax accrual net worth (see Chapter 10). This establishes value on a real number that reflects the cost of doing business.

2   Any goodwill premium, payable to the founders for their risk and reduced takeout in making the firm what it is, is formulated as a one-time premium for the founders only, and paid by the firm as additional deferred compensation or royalties.

3   Compensation of owners is divided into three categories:

   (a) Base salary.

   (b) Profit sharing—ideally a stipulated goal, based on a percentage of salary. (See Chapter 7). This allows owners and nonowners to share in initial profit distribution.

   (c) Net earnings, distributed as excess compensation to owners in proportion to their interest.

4   Buyers buy into the firm on the following basis:

   (a) The equivalent cash basis book value of the interest they are buying (calculated on the cash method of accounting) is paid into the firm in cash at the time of purchase. This is usually about one fifth to one tenth of the accrual value. It is wise to require employee buyers to find or borrow personally the necessary cash, since this gives them an invested stake in the interest, albeit a small one.

   (b) The balance of the accrued value of the interest at time of purchase is "earned" over time by the buyer forfeiting some of the profit share and net earnings compensation to which he or she would otherwise be entitled. This forfeiture (say 50% of profit share each year) continues until the full value of the interest has been left in the firm. The "forfeited" value is then distributed to the other owners, pro rata, as additional compensation as the new buyer vests the value of their interest.

5   Upon retirement (or death or disability, according to the way the plan is structured) sellers receive the formulated value of their interest as deferred compensation payable to them or their estates over 10 years.

6   The penalty for early withdrawal (prior to say, age 55)) is that sellers can redeem their interest only at the cash basis value. Thus a successor who has "earned" the accrual value of the interest on paper only cannot run off with it unless he or she stays with the firm long enough to retire.

7   All the other provisions listed on item 4 on page 142 also apply.

The value of a deferred compensation approach to paying out retiring/ withdrawing owners is that the firm can expense the payments currently and the recipient can spread the income over many years for tax purposes. This is an excellent deal for the firm and the succeeding owners. The seller takes the risk, however, that the firm may fall on bad times and be unable to complete the payments. This risk can be compensated for by valuing the long-term payout at the firm's per-tax accrual book value. The elimination of the 50% tax on the value makes the difference attractive. Perhaps the greatest merit of the approach is the burden it places on the sellers to chose successors in whom they have sufficient confidence so that the risk is worth taking. If the goal of the sellers is to perpetuate the practice, this is the most important ingredient of the whole transaction.

A WORD ABOUT INSURANCE

It is easy to be beguiled by a format for selling the firm that sets a high value (especially when that value is three or four times the net worth) and then provides insurance to cover it in recognition that the firm would be strapped, or even wiped out, if it had to pay that value to a founder's estate out of assets. Such plans look great on paper until one realizes that they are in fact nothing more than life insurance. The

Internal Revenue Service considers them to be such by not allowing tax deductions for the insurance premium unless the proceeds are paid to the firm, where they become taxable when paid to the seller's estate.

There is no free lunch. So-called key-man life insurance can have real value in insuring a firm against the untimely loss of a real producer during his or her productive years. This can be covered very inexpensively by term insurance up to, say, age 55. After age 55, if the firm does not have a plan to replace the key person's value, no insurance payment can compensate for the long-term loss. And key persons can purchase their own life insurance out of their own income on exactly the same terms as it can be passed through to them via an insured buy-sell agreement. In fact, in some cases it is better from a tax standpoint to purchase such insurance personally.

Insurance companies are in the business of selling insurance—at a profit to them. Insuring the equity value of a firm so that it will pay out on retirement is just an ingenious way to sell insurance. There are many good reasons to carry insurance, but in general they don't have a thing to do with sound ownership transition.

TAX MANIPULATIONS

Astute readers may have noted that little has been said about income tax/estate tax considerations, which have considerable impact on the final form of most organization buy-sell plans. This is not an oversight. It is fully recognized that business-based criteria combined with astute tax-planning can play a role in shaping an ownership transition plan, and tax advisors should be consulted once the framework of a desired plan is developed. But it has been the author's experience that tax/business considerations, when made paramount in a transition plan, eventually conflict with the aspects that produce the strongest succession in a design firm. The latter should always be the goal of management, because perpetuation planning is a basic function of management. It is the prerogative of owners to choose to ignore good management and go for the highest economic return at the expense of strong successors. But don't do it in the name of good management.

FIVE

HAVING THE ANSWERS IS NOT NECESSARILY THE ANSWER

Chapter 12

MANAGER OR MANAGEMENT?

"He used to be the designer—and a pretty good one. Now I don't know what he's doing. He's the president I guess."

Peter A. Piven, AIA
General Manager
Geddes Brecher Qualls Cunningham

I f managing a design firm effectively requires all that has been discussed, what happens if the talented design professional(s) who started the firm don't want to manage? What if they would rather continue doing what they do best and not "lay down their tools" to run an organization?

Obviously, this is a choice. There is nothing that compels a design professional to become a manager. Some who choose to continue in primarily "hands-on" roles keep their practices small so the management burden remains in scale with the time and energy they are willing to devote to it. Others who aspire to greater things and are successful at landing larger projects can develop fairly large organizations that function around the tasks at hand with little or no serious management. These organizations tend to suffer many of the management ills described earlier in this book, but they continue to survive as long as they fulfill the needs of their leaders. Every professional is entitled to choose whether or not he or she wishes to manage their practice, as long as the consequences of nonmanagement are accepted.

However, if the choice is to manage the organization, there are alternatives to doing it all by oneself. Management is first of all a process, not just a role, and within certain limits it is entirely possible to have an organization managed while its leaders continue to work with their tools.

To understand the choice, it is first necessary to understand the makeup of the Renaissance "whole professional" created in our design schools and by our professional registration process. The "whole" professional can perform all the functions necessary to being an architect or engineer and might be described graphically as in Figure 1.

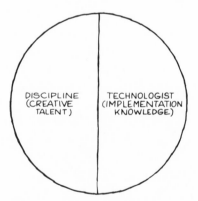

DISCIPLINE (CREATIVE TALENT)   TECHNOLOGIST (IMPLEMENTATION KNOWLEDGE)

Figure 1   The "whole" professional.

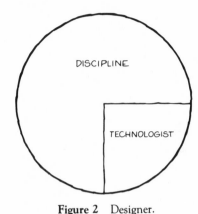

Figure 2   Designer.   Figure 3   Director of production.

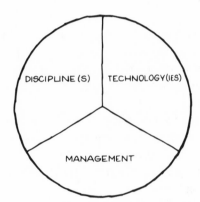

Figure 4   "Whole" professional firm.

The true Renaissance person is assumed to have these resources in some kind of equal balance. In practice of course, professionals come in a variety of complexions, depending on the role emphasis. Some typical variations are shown in Figures 2 and 3.

The professional variations are endless, and when one factors in differences in life style (ranging from the workaholic to the dilettante), there are as many varieties of the "whole" professional as there are people.

The same holds true for design organizations. The theoretical complete design firm will have a Renaissance balance of discipline talent, technological expertise, and management attention (Figure 4).

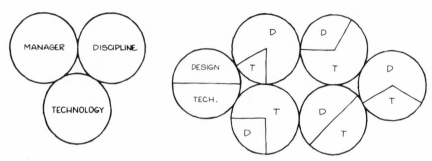

Figure 5 Specialists creating a whole firm.

Figure 6 Varied individuals creating a whole firm.

In the firm context, however, this balance of inputs is provided in a variety of ways depending on the aptitudes and choices of the individuals.

Perhaps the purest format is for one individual to specialize wholly in each area of the firm (Figure 5).

But since this is neither the way professionals are made nor the way they like to work, the typical design organization tends to be an amalgam of different individuals, as in Figure 6.

In one approach to managing this system one of the group can assume primary responsibility for management, as in Figure 7. The authority and responsibility are then very clear. The disadvantage is that one of the group must give up his or her tools, and the others must agree to be managed by that person.

Another approach (Figure 8) is for each of the participants to accept some responsibility for management in addition to their other roles. This has the advantage of allowing all of the players to continue practicing their profession, and it gives each of the key people an opportunity to contribute to management. The disadvantage is in its potential for cumbersome and compromised decision making, and resulting inefficiency.

Whether the system shown in Figure 8 can work depends largely on the personal styles of the firm's individuals. If they work well together, have mutual respect, are willing to live with delegated decisions, and can be constructively confrontive when disagreements do arise, there is every reason to expect shared management should work.

In many firms with shared management, however, these factors are lacking. Then, as management issues become progressively more uncom-

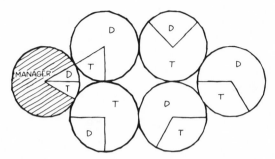

Figure 7   One-manager approach.

fortable, each player concentrates more and more on his or her project/
discipline tasks, and less time is devoted to the concerns of the organization. The result is undermanagement, the leading cause of distress in
design organization.

It is a worthwhile exercise to budget the amount of management
time required to keep an organization running well, and then keep
timecard records of the time actually devoted to management by the
principals. As a rule of thumb, the sum of management and marketing
time in a healthy design firm will be about 10% of total personnel time,
and at least half of that management time must be top−management
(principal) time and not just delegated effort by a controller, personnel
manager, or other subordinate. This means that the full-time equivalent
of one principal/manager/marketer is required for every 20 persons on the
staff.

Many design organizations do not have the capacity for so much
management within the control. group—hence the prevalence of un-

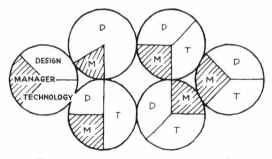

Figure 8   Shared management approach.

dermanagement. One alternative being tried by a small but growing number of firms is to hire a trained general manager to fill some of the functions the principals are neglecting. A typical job description for a general manager with full-time management as his or her primary role is included as Appendix 1. To date, however, most firms have been delegating management tasks bit by bit, rather than to one general manager. This practice has been particularly prevalent in the financial and marketing areas. It remains to be seen whether professional staffs will respond positively to human resource specialists who come aboard to deal with issues of motivation and career development or to expediters who ride herd on project schedules and budgets without regard for quality judgments. So long as the objective of the staff in executing the firm's projects is professional performance, it is likely that the staff will respond best to management by other professionals whom they consider their peers or mentors.

A more promising trend is the growing number of student architects and engineers who are taking graduate training in management (MBAs) before going into practice. Some of the technical schools have even begun to offer joint master's degrees in architecture or engineering and business management. The development of design professionals committed to management as part of their career path may in time solve the management dilemma in design practice.

It is more likely, however, that the architects and engineers who rise to the top of their fields and go into private practice will continue to be those who are the most talented professionals in their discipline—not the best managers. For them it will be of little help, but of some consolation, to know that their instincts to be task oriented and to undermanage their firms are widely shared and have been characteristic of professional firms for generations.

From that point onward, the degree to which they succeed in installing management in their organizations will be a matter of choice. No one can require an organization to be well managed. The level of management at the bottom line in every design practice will always be subject to the same qualitative judgments that set the standard of professional performance. This, in fact, is the way other professionals, particularly lawyers, accountants, and doctors, have practiced for years.

Architects and engineers who consider the field primarily as a business may continue to strive to treat their practices like a business. But those who think of design practice as a true profession will do best if they manage their affairs in a professional format. This may not be as efficient, tightly controlled, or tidily structured as the management textbooks say it ought to be, but it will be professionally satisfying and personally rewarding.

Isn't that the real bottom bottom line?

Appendix 1

JOB AND PERSON DESCRIPTION FOR A GENERAL MANAGER

POSITION	General Manager
REPORTS TO	(Board or Partnership)
GENERAL DESCRIPTION	Assists the Board/Partnership in the formulation of long-range goals for the firm and is responsible for devising and implementing strategies for their achievement.
SPECIFIC DUTIES	Direct and control the firm's day-to-day affairs by establishing operating objectives, formulating policies, programs, and procedures designed to attain these objectives, and monitoring progress toward their achievement.

Communicate the firm's objectives and policies to all employees. Ensure that all personnel in the firm are utilized in the most efficient and productive way possible, taking full advantage of their individual talents and providing opportunities for personnel to acquire new skills and broader responsibilities as they are able.

Assign functions and tasks necessary to achieve the firm's goals to organizational components and to individual employees. Establish procedures for accountability reporting and set the pattern for internal relationships to be observed by all members of the organization.

Assist the Marketing Director in the formulation of an overall business development program including identification of target markets, appropriate communication tools, public relations activities, new services, marketing budget requirements and manpower needs, scheduling, interview strategies, and coordination of overall effort.

Monitor performance of firm's project leaders to ensure that work is produced consistently through the adopted process, is of high quality, is responsive to the client's needs, and meets fee, schedule, and construction budget constraints.

Supervise the preparation and negotiation of all contracts; establish procedures to keep on top of changes in scope of work that should result in revisions to agreements and additional payments.

Establish a philosophy of, and overall requirements for, an effective financial information system; develop firmwide budgeting and reporting systems.

Through the controller, produce periodic analysis of the financial position of the firm; review financial performance against budgeted objectives; note any significant deviations from sound financial planning; develop and recommend appropriate corrective action where necessary.

Monitor all overhead expenditures and take corrective action when necessary to achieve the firm's profit planning objectives.

See that adequate funds are maintained to meet current and future operations.

Counsel key executives on levels of compensation appropriate to the levels of responsibility and contribution of their subordinates.

Direct the development of standard policies and procedures, special manuals and forms.

Report regularly to the Board/Partners on progress toward achievement of the firm's goals.

Recommend to the Board of Directors guidelines for the distribution and retention of profits resulting from the firm's operations.

PERSONAL
QUALITIES

Sensitivity to people.

Track record in people management.

Self-starter.

Aggressive, but gentle and direct.

Creative problem solver.

Polished social skills.

Appendix 2

JOB AND PERSON DESCRIPTION FOR A MARKETING DIRECTOR/MANAGER

POSITION	Director/Manager of Marketing

POSITION Director/Manager of Marketing

REPORTS TO (Board/Partnership/or General Manager)

EXTENT OF JOB Under the general direction of management, plans and coordinates all marketing activities of the firm. Responsibilities involve developing and executing a marketing program which consists of establishing long-range marketing goals and near-term objectives; selecting target markets; and, in close coordination with the principals, screening leads, contacting and cultivating prospects, and obtaining contracts for projects.

SPECIFIC DUTIES

Planning • Has major responsibility for developing and executing a Marketing Plan which outlines all major aspects of a planned marketing effort including appropriate objectives, tasks, assignments of responsibility to individuals and budgets. The Marketing Plan is to be developed in coordination with the principles approved by management. The remaining specific duties are to be performed within the framework of the marketing plan.

Market Direction • Determine what specific markets the firm will cultivate. The determination will be made after careful appraisal of the likely market opportunities for the firm.

Targeting • Establish, for each market where active new business effort is to be applied, specific performance goals for the subsequent twelve months. These goals should include:

(a) The number of new organizations to be contacted during the year.

(b) Where applicable, the number of follow-up calls to be made on former clients or prior contacts.

(c) The number of anticipated interviews with prospects who are actively considering selection of professional services.

(d) The desired volume of commissions and total gross fees to be realized from the sales effort in this market.

Lead Developing

- Operating directly or through designated staff personnel, develop lists of individuals and/or projects (leads/prospects) to be contacted. Organize and screen leads/prospects to produce an efficient procedure for scheduling contacts. Ensure that appropriate individuals are assigned, scheduled, and equipped to make the desired business development contacts.

Strategy Development

- Develop strategies for cultivating prospects and obtaining work at the target market, individual prospect, and project levels. Play a coordinating role in preparing content for interviews and presentations, including determining the level of participation by other staff personnel. Take primary responsibility for coordinating proposals, pricing, and response strategy.

Client Maintenance

- Keep abreast of the progress of projects and see that the firm maintains a continuing relationship with clients during the course of and after the completion of assignments—including project oriented public relations activities.

Sales Tools

- Take primary responsibility for determining what materials and

information are needed, coordinating the
production of such materials and
information. This will include proposals,
graphics, brochures, presentation
materials, the U.S. Gov't #254, business
development oriented correspondence,
etc.

Merchandising and   • Develop a plan for appropriate advertising
Public Relations   and/or public relations activities to
                               support the firms's marketing program,
                               and see that appropriate staff or
                               consultants are retained to carry it out.

Monitoring   • Maintain (directly or through designated
                               staff personnel) a record and control
                               system to alert appropriate individuals
                               when contacts are to be made; and to
                               serve as a log to record all marketing
                               activities.

                               Maintain (directly or through designated
                               staff personnel) a control system to
                               measure the performance of the marketing
                               effort; and an activity review system for
                               management.

Marketing Staff   • With the approval of management, hire or
                               obtain the services of others to help carry
                               out the marketing functions.

General   • Keep abreast of issues and current trends
                               in the marketplace and the profession
                               likely to affect the firm and its marketing
                               activities.

PERSONAL   Ability to plan and organize.
QUALITIES
                             Communicates well with others both in
                             face-to-face and in group meetings.

Flexible, readily adaptable to changing conditions and demands.

Self-confident and not easily discouraged.

Able to relate to client and client's concerns and interests. Interested in public and community activities.

Creative, problem-solving approach to work and a facility to generate new ideas and build on the ideas of others.

Appendix 3

JOB AND PERSON DESCRIPTION FOR A LEAD FINDER

POSITION	Lead Finder

REPORTS TO   Director of Marketing

EXTENT OF JOB   Coordinates and monitors on-going contacts and communications between staff and new business leads and prospects. Searches out, identifies and establishes initial contact with leads in new business situations and markets, and assists in client relations with current and past clients. Establishes rapport, monitors and maintains communications, and elicits such information from prospects to allow development of strategy for a successful marketing team approach.

SPECIFIC DUTIES

List Building
- Develop lead lists from various sources suitable to firm markets and potential volume.

Contacting
- Establish contact with leads and elicit such information as to the type of project, dollar volume, schedule, method of financing, decision-making process, decision-maker(s), and other pertinent information. Also coordinate and monitor lead development activities of the staff that may overlap.

Strategy Development
- Based on indicated information, develop strategy that is most promising to present the firm and win project. In concert with Director of Marketing, develop most appropriate marketing team for presentations and formal interviews. Responsible for assembling group and meshing their schedules with those of the project.

Interface
- In addition to client contact for new business development, assist in the

researching and preparation of sales presentations. Make effective handoff to members of the marketing team.

Communications

- Internal - Keep Director of Marketing appraised through regularly scheduled reports of actions, schedules and potential prospects.

  External - Responsible for coordination of submittals to prospects of all information necessary to reinforce the firms's position, i.e., brochures, 254-255 Forms, articles, leaving pieces, strong "selling" letters, etc.

Market Research

- Keep knowledgeable of all aspects of the profession and current trends in assigned markets. Make special marketing surveys, as required.

PERSONAL QUALITIES

- Confident, poised, ambitious. Not easily discouraged by rejection.

  Able to collect, analyze, communicate and act on client data.

  Energetic, a doer. Responsive to the firm and able to convey that enthusiasm to potential clients. Warm, open personality. Not dogmatic or inflexible. Readily adaptable to changing condition or demands.

  Creative problem-solver; likely to try several approaches when initial solution fails.

Appendix 4

JOB AND PERSON DESCRIPTION FOR A MARKETING COORDINATOR

POSITION	Marketing Coordinator
EXTENT OF JOB	Coordinate marketing, market research and public relations activities of the firm, under the direction of the (Marketing Director or General Manager) and working closely with all principals. Responsibilities include support of the principals of the firm in their individual lead finding and selling efforts; monitoring the progress of all marketing efforts; organizing the development of all administrative systems and selling tool resources.

SPECIFIC DUTIES

Market Research

- Assist in identifying contacts for sources of market research information and preparing questions to be used in research interviews; compile data gathered during research interviews; help interpret results of research and apply them to lead finding and selling efforts.

Contact Lists

- Assist in developing principals' individual lists of contracts in target markets; transfer raw data into a format for the organization and maintenance of lists; administer annual review of lists to add and delete names and correct data.

Lead Finding

- Assist principals in scheduling contacts and preparing for sales calls; record data and follow-up recommendations, prepare follow-up materials as required, maintain follow-up schedule and assist in the preparation of correspondence.

Response

- As leads are identified, assist principals in planning, coordinating and conducting strategy research efforts; assist in preparing materials for credentials submittals, presentations and proposals.

Selling Operations
- Monitor effectiveness of selling effort and secure feedback from prospects regardless of outcomes. Maintain all marketing paperwork systems including call reports; mailing lists; screening reports; and prospect correspondence files.

Sales Tools
- Organize and maintain photographic, slide and proposal files and data on the credentials of the firm; assist in the development of brochure materials.

Public Relations
- Assist in the development and coordination of special events and feature and routine publicity (in concert with the firm's public relations counsel, if appropriate). Identify opportunities for placement of articles and publicity in professional journals, magazines, and newspapers. Possibly, develop and prepare a periodic firm newsletter.

General
- Remain in close contact with principals on business development, giving input and guidance as necessary. Perform other marketing and public relations duties as requested by the principals.

PERSONAL QUALITIES

Well-organized and self-disciplined.

Persistent and assertive but not abrasive.

Excellent writing abilities.

Ability to communicate well with others.

Graphic design sensitivity and taste.

Public relations orientation.

INDEX